#1 BESTSELLING AUTHOR

DANIELLE WURTH

IGNITE
THE ORGANIZER IN YOUR CHILD

Developing the Life Skills Required
To Thrive at Home, School, and Beyond

Niche Pressworks

IGNITE THE ORGANIZER IN YOUR CHILD

ISBN 978-1-946533-80-7 (paperback)

ISBN 978-1-946533-77-7 (ebook)

Copyright © 2020 by Danielle Wurth

All rights reserved. No part of this publication may be reproduced, stored in a retrieval system, or transmitted in any form or by any means – for example, electronic, photocopying, recording – without the prior written permission of Wurth Organizing, LLC, except as provided by the United States of America copyright law. The only exception is brief quotations in printed book reviews.

For permission to reprint portions of this content or bulk purchases, contact Wurth Organizing, LLC at WurthOrganizing.com

Published by Niche Pressworks; http://NichePressworks.com

Dedication

To my beautiful, loving, supportive family: Philly My Love; Devon and Oliver; Diana, Mom and Ken; Dad and Patti. Every single family member has shown me such incredible encouragement over the years while working on this book. I will forever cherish all our heartfelt talks and cheers that have happened throughout the years.

Contents

Dedication iii

Foreword by Dr. Lynne Kenney, Psy.D. ix

Preface xiii

Matters of the Heart

1. Ignite Your Child's Organizing Personality 3

   What is YOUR CHILD'S Organizing Personality? 8

2. Bust Out and Build Your Organizing Tool Kit Together 19

Matters of the Mind

3. When a Master Gatekeeper Trains a Domain Defender 29

4. Become a Master Decision-Making Duo 43

5. Kicking Ace: Mastering the Four A's of Organizing Together 51

   Epic Organizing Adventure: Toy Virus Take Down 54

6. Empower Your Children, Not Enable Them™ 61

   Epic Organizing Adventure: Increasing Attention to Detail 65

   Epic Organizing Adventure: Manners to Model After 74

7. How to R.O.C.K. at Discipline 77

   Handling Meltdowns 82

   Epic Organizing Adventure: R.O.C.K. Method Activities 84

8. **Daily Systems and Rhythms** 87

9. **Kids' Rooms: Natural Disaster or Comforting Shelter** 97

10. **Toys, Trinkets, and Treasures** 125

11. **Conquer Art, Medals, and Memory Mayhem** 137

12. **Creating Homework Zones** 143

    Epic Organizing Adventure: Homework Contract Completion 145

13. **Kids in the Kitchen** 153

    Meal Planning: Make it Simple and Savory 162

14. **Laundry Load Line Up: How Kids Can Tackle It** 171

Matters of Reference

15. The Coaching Corner: A Few Quick Wins to Conquer Anytime 181

    Resource Guide 187

    A Thousand Thanks 191

    Acknowledgements 192

    About the Author 193

Foreword
By Dr. Lynne Kenney, Psy.D.

Your home is a sanctuary for your family. It is the place in which you all wish to relax, revive, and thrive. While most of us desire an organized family home, many of us do not know how to achieve it. Danielle Wurth's *Ignite the Organizer in Your Child* provides the keys to helping you and your child develop the skills to create the home you always wanted. A home in which there is a place for everything. A home that is uncluttered, yet full of the personal touches that make it your own.

Creating your organized home is a family affair involving everyone: most importantly your child. Raising a child with good organizational skills is beneficial not only for the well-being of your family, but for the life skills of your child. Children who are organized know how to approach tasks, complete actions, and follow through in activities of daily living, homework, sports, and work life.

The challenge that many children face, particularly young children, is that their brains are not mature enough to process complex instructions. So, you may tell them, "Hey, when you walk in the door, hang up your coat, tap the dirt off your boots, and bring your backpack to your homework station." But what their growing brains may think instead is, "Grab the Xbox before your brother gets it." And everything gets thrown on the couch, including the muddy boots.

Danielle and her team have worked with over a thousand families, and she gets it. She understands that the prefrontal cortex, which houses the organizational centers of our brains, is developing until we are young adults and, in gifted children, continues to fully develop into their early thirties.

In order to help the brains of her clients, she teaches them metacognitive skills: planning, decision-making, and time management. Her organizing methods are a delicate blend of collaborative parenting, teaching, and organizational strategies. Danielle is doing more than helping your child learn how to lead an organized life; she is teaching you and your child the skills to think better, to live better.

Ignite the Organizer in Your Child will help your child develop the cognitive skills needed to be a successful, social human being and will help you, as a parent, to raise one. The book includes easy-to-follow checklists and printables that aid in previewing what it looks like to declutter, decide, and collectively manage a happy, healthy home.

Danielle takes you through step-by-step actions in a humorous, yet informative way to help you raise an organized child by ...

- Discovering your child's unique organizing personality.
- Learning how to introduce a life-altering organization style to your home and family.
- Developing strategies that don't simply initiate the organization process, but help your child maintain organized spaces, eventually doing so on their own.
- Creating a system for your child's schoolwork, artwork, and keepsakes.
- Building cognitive and learning skills in your child that will benefit him his entire life.
- Discovering how to deepen the relationship with your child using Danielle's R.O.C.K. parenting technique.

With *Ignite the Organizer in Your Child*, your family life will immediately improve as your focus shifts from frustration and chaos to calm cooperation with shared goals, respect, and love.

DR. LYNNE KENNEY, PSY.D.,

Pediatric Psychologist and International Educator

Author of *Bloom Your Room; Musical Thinking; and Bloom: 50 Things to Say, Think, and Do with Anxious, Angry, and Over-the-Top Kids (Kenney & Young, 2015).*

PREFACE

I chose the word IGNITE when naming my book specifically because it conveys my mission for both the parent and child. Each chapter will teach how to nurture your child's own flame, which, in turn, will evoke permanent change in how you will assist them in overcoming organizing challenges. Igniting their organizing flame is the first step in that chain reaction that will transform their life.

IGNITE - verb

transitive verb

1a: to set a fire: KINDLE

b: to cause (a fuel) to burn

2: to subject to fire or intense heat

3a: to heat up: EXCITE

b: to set in motion: SPARK *ignite* a debate *intransitive verb*

1: to catch fire

2: to begin to glow[1]

---

[1] Merriam-Webster, s.v. "ignite," https://www.merriam-webster.com/dictionary/ignite.

MATTERS
— OF THE —
HEART

IGNITE YOUR CHILD'S ORGANIZING PERSONALITY

The love for a child is so powerful—whether your journey started from that unforgettable day they were born, adopted into your family, or through fostering. Each day, you work tirelessly with courage and compassion to provide a home environment for them to thrive into their full potential. Some days can cause gut-wrenching frustration, while others are glorious beyond belief ... and all the while, you and your child learn more about yourselves and each other.

Whether or not you've kindly been granted natural-born organizing *skills* as the parent, it is likely your organizing *style* may differ from your child's ... Welcome to Parent Land, where the family adventures begin, and the need for exploration and excitement never ends! Your child wants to *venture left* using one set of organizing solutions (or lack thereof), while you want to *venture right* because it seems like the more logical choice for them. By joining together, communicating, and clarifying the desires you both crave, collectively you can lean on and learn from one another, ultimately finding an entirely new path straight ahead.

> **"Organizing is as much a *discovery* process
> as it is a *recovery* process."™**

This powerful concept is one I shared in my foundational book *Ignite the Organizer in You*. I feel that the earlier in life a parent introduces organizing, the more beneficial it will be and the more impact it will have on children being raised in this complicated, ever-changing world.

I believe that once you *discover* an area in your child where they naturally show strong interest (e.g., clothes, crafts, games), then you can work with them to transfer those skills to a larger organizing project. Doing this will allow them to shift their mindset and *recover* from feeling frustrated and defeated in areas where they may not be "naturally" gifted.

Focusing on these interests can help transform their habits into healthier and more intentional organizing behaviors. The process of looking at what currently exists within your child and then envisioning a better future, that's the spark you need to start. Once you take that newfound "spark" and gently "fan it into a flame," then BAM … a blaze develops, and you have *Ignited the Organizer in Your Child*.

In *Ignite the Organizer in You,* I had you ponder on an area in *your* life where you *naturally* had a strong interest. Now it is time to apply the same thought process by pondering on an area in your *child's life* where they *naturally* have a strong interest. Think of a particular activity or hobby where they are independently and deeply engaged.

For some children, this may mean hand selecting pieces for an outfit or meticulously finding the perfect materials to complete a homework project or creating detailed strategies to beat an opponent in their favorite video game. These are areas that are important *to them* which, in turn, makes them equally as important *to you* as their parent or caregiver.

Just like any important project which requires support, organizing requires that same kind of common foundation in order to turn your home into a loving family home instead of opposing military forces with NERF® guns in hand. Instead of firing shots *toward* each other, you work together as a team to *support* each other. It is equally important to study your child as you would a spouse. **When you discover what *matters* to them, you will uncover what *motivates* them to achieve it.**

Taking the time (and some emotional self-control) to reveal these core truths is critical to a trusting and loving parent/child relationship where everyone can thrive rather than just survive at home together.

Let me tell you a story of how organizing led a practicing Child Psychologist Mother and her 10-year-old daughter to move from a state of constant "clean up your bedroom" battles to having a huge relationship breakthrough that changed everything. Not only was I able to alter the daughter's behavior in a few sessions, but also assisted them in selecting organizing solutions ...all via Skype!

Even though the daughter excelled strongly in school and sports, the mother was frustrated that the daughter "never cleaned her room." However, the daughter was equally frustrated that she didn't have a room that reflected her personality or one that had enough space and solutions to organize her belongings.

This clean-your-bedroom battle went back and forth over the years, causing each side to take a strong stance in their relationship (imagine NERF gun bullets of bickering words flying here, there, and everywhere!). I talked privately with the mom about her top desires for the room, and then had a private conversation with the daughter about her needs. To my surprise, they BOTH wanted the same thing ... a well-organized room and a better relationship!

The issue was: the mother didn't really take the time to *"discover the spark,"* which was important to the daughter in transforming her space. The daughter's needs were pretty straightforward: new paint for the walls, more color in general, a modern vibe to the decor, furniture that was age-appropriate, a new hamper of appropriate size, a reading nook that doubled as a homework area, and a sleepover space for friends.

Once we *assessed* the space and its function and *attacked* what was to stay and what should go, we were ready to *assign* a solution based on the floorplan and accessories we discussed would work. They ventured off for a shopping trip to IKEA™. They called me shortly after, literally gushing in girlie excitement—not just about what they found, but also about how wonderful and memorable the day had been since they had the same plan and purpose.

From that day forward, their relationship was forever changed. Their words, not mine. The mother later confided in me that she now realized that she never really "knew" her daughter and how all of us collaborating together in this organizing experience had been so impactful to both of them. Organizing is THAT powerful. And that is my sole purpose for writing this book.

In my mind and heart, stewarding and organizing go hand-in-hand. The foundation of this belief comes from my faith and the stewardship concept represented in the Parable of the Talents, Matthew 25:14–28. The Lord entrusts us to steward, honor, and respect what he has given us. So, with that being said, I visualize a "cross" on every single item I own and convey this concept to my boys, as well. From the markers on their homework station to the clothes in their closet and the sports equipment in the garage. In this spirit, the things the Lord has blessed our family with will become a blessing to others once again.

This little book is like me sharing all my endless organizing secrets, tips and systems so both you and your child can take tremendous strides to move forward versus stumbling sideways in frustration. I am so very excited because of all of the amazing things that are on the verge of happening to YOU BOTH! Woohoo!

This approach to organizing will not force your child to strip themselves of all their favorite belongings to conform with an extreme minimalist ethic, but they will also not be allowed to store endless years of all their artwork and outgrown toy sets in nifty, labeled, matching containers, stacked taller than they are.

Instead, this is the type of organizing book where we'll work together to develop and define that "sweet spot" in the middle of both mindsets that represents you and your family values. Our work will fan the flame in your child, so you can watch it glow.

In the first section of the book, *Matters of the Heart*, you will define your child's Organizing Personality and how it relates to them as a student. Then, in the second section, *Matters of the Mind*, new perspectives will be revealed about being mindful of *what* they own and what its *purpose* is in their life.

In a future section, *Matters of the Hands,* you will be guided through transforming core spaces in your family abode, while learning how to work together on tasks and life skills that can be adjusted to be age-appropriate

Finally, you will learn how to become more productive and efficient as a parent once certain systems are established and expectations for your child are set accordingly. The days of experiencing frustrated parent fails will be old news. You will never again doubt that you can spark the inner organizer fire inside your child. NEVER! Instead, let's light it up people and start discovering their Organizing Personality!

What is YOUR CHILD'S Organizing Personality?

As a professional organizer and mother, I find it very useful to label as much as possible. Not only does a label "do the speaking for you" as the parent, but, in turn, your child can feel proudly independent in completing daily tasks on their own. Although parents tend to shy away from wanting to "label" their child's behaviors, I think it's really helpful to visualize the current challenges, while envisioning possible future changes. The same goes for understanding your child's Organizing Personality and how it relates to them as a student and their personal space. Where are they putting things, and why? Why are they behaving a certain way when it comes to organizing related responsibilities?

Let's begin by having fun reflecting on children's behaviors around their "stuff and systems." Following are some lighthearted labels to which you can relate.

Before I dive into it all, let me share that each personality has its own strengths! My job and the role of this book is to help you better understand and appreciate WHY your child loves what they love, how it represents them, and what no longer serves a purpose in the current stage of their home, school, and current stage of life.

Each child's organizing personality dictates how a child relates to *what* they own and the *meaning* behind it. I have worked with nearly every type of child personality. They truthfully don't depart too much from the adult Organizing Personalities I discussed in my first book, *Ignite the Organizer in You*. The sooner you can identify which type of Organizing Personality your child has, the more successful you will be in transitioning and transforming their life into healthier organizing habits. Today, it's their room. Tomorrow it's their dorm, then first apartment, and lastly their own family nest.

Let's see what you discover about your kiddo! It may not be too far from your own Organizing Personality. Or, perhaps it's the complete opposite, which may shed some light on how you relate to one another's needs and values ... oh-so-interesting. Sound like a game plan to go for?

From this moment forward you have officially moved into a no-guilt parent zone. Yes! There is no reason to waste today's current emotions and energies on decisions made in the past. That is what is soooo great about time. It literally has a beginning *and* end—every day! Ready to roll out a new day? I know I am, so let's find out which of these personalities bests describes YOUR CHILD.

Grab your kiddo, snuggle together, and read them all out loud with a humorous heart. Remember, you are reading this book as a *guide* and not a *judge*, so be extra aware of your emotional tone during this quality time together. Adjust wording to be age-appropriate so they can decide what *they* feel describes them best. I am notorious for "snack bribing" my boys into activities they are reluctant to try. I also require kisses when my extra awesomeness needs to be acknowledged. I LOVE to make literally ANYTHING more fun! And remember, ***happy days come through organized ways!*** ™

The Clock Chaser

The schedule of your daily life is running you ragged. You don't have enough time between school, sports, and extracurricular activities to push the pause button and catch up on unfinished work and responsibilities. If you and your parent don't find a way to slow down your schedule, you both are going to miss building important critical thinking skills, personal growth skills, and organizing life skills.

Being overcommitted outside the home has led you to be under-committed inside the home. There is no time for you to put away your laundry and toys or to tidy up your room so you can feel proud of it and show off to your friends. Nor is there time to complete unfinished projects, such as creating organizing solutions for past schoolwork, memory keepsakes, or treasure boxes of past birthday party trinkets.

Tell your parent you would like to talk about not doing some outside activities so you can make time and space for what you own. It takes time to figure out what you need to keep and what to do with it all. Learning to make choices about which things matter will help you be confident and build core organizing skills to help you succeed in school and everyday life.

The Creative Collector

You are a lover of all things unique, crafty, and creative. Your heart is compelled to *gather* because *things* bring you HUGE joy and special memories. But your "joyful collections" have taken over open space in your desk, drawers, and closet. Not cool. If only you had a bigger room! Your parent's solution is to purchase more organizing things to store your "collections," but now you don't have much room to play either. You eventually will need a zip line to fly across your room if you want to have a playdate with friends. Whee!

It's time for you to review your "collections" and keep only your most favorite, favorite, favorite things. You likely are a very caring, sensitive spirit, which is what makes you so special! It will make *you* smile super big to see *other* kids smile super big when you pass some of your things along to them. Tell your parents how *hard* it is for you to let things go and keep your room clean and orderly. They understand this important skill you need to learn and will listen to your caring heart. But you can learn to make mindful choices. Mastering decision-making today will help you avoid poor decisions tomorrow—on homework, projects, and selecting friends of good character.

The Game Changer

You kept all your toys and clothes organized in your room, and then something changed: you moved houses, your family foundation shifted, or you just grew up. Just like games change to different levels, so did your life. And *clothes and hobbies* were part of that shift. Now, your organizing *systems* need to *change* to a different level too.

Sometimes there are situations in a family's life where there isn't the extra time or money for projects. This is common. Share your new interests with your parent and talk about needs for your space. Create a plan to work together to make some changes happen!

Maybe you once enjoyed playing with your American Girl® doll sets, but now, you'd rather have a dressing table area to do your hair and paint nails with friends. Or maybe LEGO® building was once your jam, but now your focus is on robotics, so you need table space and specific lighting for it.

Suggest items you can help clean, organize, and sell, with the proceeds going toward your new hobbies. It may take longer than you wanted to get everything done. But helping your parent through the transition process will be such a cool organizing experience, and you'll be proud to show it off to your friends when it's finished!

The Secretive Stuffer

You desperately desire to be an organized person. It would be totally epic to get it all sorted out and labeled nicely someday. But then, you ask, "Where would I start?" The idea of an organized room sounds amazing, but the work would be wayyyy too overwhelming. You weren't born with natural, God-given organizing skills, nor were you taught them in a way that worked for you while growing up. Your solution is to be a "stuffer," and scoop up all your "stuff" into any open drawer or bin.

Prior to friends and family visiting, you are told to "clean your room." Your go-to solution is "stuffing," since you don't have any organization solutions in place. Clean clothes keep getting mixed with dirty clothes because there isn't room in your drawers, closets, or hamper to put them. Toy and tech sets are all mixed up too. Everyone thinks you are so organized, but you know that you just "stuff away your stuff."

It's time to stop living in secret and start stewarding your belongings better. Share with your parents how long it takes to find what you need when you need it, and how everything is just so mixed up and confusing. When you are able to tackle your space together, you'll find a massive pressure has been lifted. It will look and feel so clean everywhere. You won't be able to stop opening and closing your drawers, peeking at everything folded neatly, and by color. Now, you will be able to have fun (and not be stressed) getting dressed for school. And this will make you and your parent oh-so-happy.

The Storm Maker

Your parent knows the paths you have traveled around the house, since tracks of your personal debris were left behind—from socks and shoes to broken chips and permission slips. Your energy is abundant, and your brain is always working, thinking, and easily distracted. You don't mean to cause a stormy mess wherever you go since it makes people upset with you, but it just keeps happening. There are so many things to think and do at once, it is hard to focus and finish one task at a time.

Share with your parent that you really are *trying*, but it often doesn't work out since tasks just take longer for you or distractions are endless. You both can learn how order will reduce your frustration and increase your confidence when things are well labeled. Taming both small and big projects will now be easier for you to finish. This fine-tuning will eventually turn those storm clouds into clear skies, giving you a clearer mind that will help you focus on moving straight ahead. If you can hone your potential organizing skills and master self-control, you can go from leaving a path of destruction to becoming a dynamically talented force in life. It is the Storm Chasers in the business world who have made some of the most powerful impacts.

The Methodical Mind

You like consistency and order. It makes logical sense to follow a simple format for organizing since it is easier to keep track of your things when you have methods in place. Even though you are naturally good at organizing, spaces in your room still don't look *complete* to you. A few drawers, shelves, and baskets work and function okay, but you know there is a better way. There are better ideas, better methods, and better solutions.

Having things labeled would be so awesome and look much better. You don't know how to use a label maker but are definitely open to learning about it with your parent. It bugs you, big time, that you have spent countless hours organizing, trying to get your space to look awesome, but it's still not happening.

Share with your parent what you think works and doesn't work in your room. Perhaps you both can discuss how to complete it. Your motivation and confidence in one another will be your greatest support to get you nearer the finish line. You both are so close to achieving it, you can practically touch it. Once you and your parent select the right products and systems, your room will be lookin' super-duper sharp. Your methodical mind will think much more clearly, and you'll be able to better focus at school and with ongoing projects.

Chaotic Cluttered Combo

You may be uber-organized at school, but not at home. You have a well-organized desk in the classroom, yet your one at home is infected with the nasty "paperwork virus." How is that possible? You may suffer from "multiple-organizing-personality disorder."

The organizing dysfunction becomes more complex when any of the above personalities combine, or if it occurs in different environments. This can strike at any time and in any combination of ways and spaces.

If this describes you, then it's time to have a serious kumbaya talk with your parent to define the more dominant dysfunctional personality. It's time to change those old chaotic habits of just putting things in random places and random ways. Imagine how amazing it will be to finally be *that* organized kid—one who is organized at school *and* is an organized family helper at home.

Ask your parent to help you discover what things are frustrating for you, and what you truly want for your personal space. Your parent will appreciate your gratitude—for what you own and for the fact that each morning, you're issued a brand spankin' new day. Time for you to stop feeling bad about past poor decisions and redirect that energy toward a new vision. Imagine the freedom! Can you feel it? Can your parent feel it? Congrats! You both are halfway there ... now go make it real.

Over the years, these are the organizing personalities I've encountered most often in children. Do you see your child in any or a few of these categories? Then, we're about to get started.

Join me in this book, and we will *Ignite the Organizer in Your Child*. I want to help you guide them to *think differently* about what they own, *why* they own it, and why it has *value* to remain with them in their current stage of life.

As I mentioned earlier, the book is purposefully divided into three supportive Pillars. I recommend you work through and incorporate the recommendations in the order presented, which avoids further confusion and delay reaching your and your child's organizing goals.

Pillar I: Matters of the Heart – teaches you how to define your Child's Organizing Personality and how to build your Organizing Tool Kit.

Pillar II: Matters of the Mind – teaches you and your child how to think like an organizer.

Pillar III: Matters of The Hands – you both will apply the above skills to organize specific spaces in your home.

It is truly essential that you read through Pillars I and II to get your heart and mind ready so the spaces discussed in Pillar III can be transformed in the most efficient manner. You have the choice to tackle *any* space in the last pillar in *any* order, but only once you have completed the foundational framework of *Pillars I and II*. The only exception is for those who crave the experience of ultimate insanity, where you take pleasure in moving in nauseating circles, like a merry-go-round at the county fair, wondering why you can't break free to experience different results.

A Stack of Clutter-Free Coins will be earned at the end of each chapter to keep your "organizing game" strategy strong. This will help you and your kiddo review your newly learned skills with a checklist and prove your readiness for the next organizing adventure.

 Keep your "organizing eyes" peeled for a Jeep icon representing **"Epic Organizing Adventure"** activities you can do with your kiddo.

Doing these together will further enforce the purpose of the activity, and be a helpful practice of certain organizing skills required. This all happens while engaging in quality time as a family. The time shall serve as both purposeful *and* productive in its own unique way.

Ready to go? Let's bring it on!

- ✓ Visit **WurthOrganizing.com** and locate the **Printables Tab** to print your set of printable pages which accompany the book's teaching methods. There is also a **Resource Guide** at the back of the book that references all the suggested products and printables for each chapter.
- ✓ If you ever feel overwhelmed, flip to the last section of the book titled ***Matters of Reference,*** where you will find ***The Coaching Corner: A Few Quick Wins to Conquer Anytime.*** These will boost your confidence level right back up!

Sign up for our *__Teachable Tips__* to receive our most clever organizing methods and moments shared with clients and kiddos just like you!

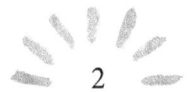

2

BUST OUT AND BUILD YOUR ORGANIZING TOOL KIT TOGETHER

Like any task, organizing requires the right tools and planning before you start. Would you start running a bath for your child with only a clean, dry towel, but no soap or shampoo? Of course not! It would be an inefficient use of time and energy to place one item in your child's bathroom, then dash to yours to find your missing items, moving from one bathroom to the next and delivering one item at a time.

Aside from the irresponsibility of leaving a bathing child unattended, it is also far more efficient to gather all bath gear necessities onto a bathroom caddy first, rather than dashing between bathrooms to find and deliver them all. Please nod your head in agreement, or I will be forced to splash icy cold water on you to wake you up … Sheesh!

We will use the same approach toward organizing. We will gather all the core products you and your child will need to create a personalized Organizing Tool Kit. It doesn't have to be perfect, and you don't need a fancy container. *It is more important to focus on gathering everything that is essential and keeping items in a single, secure place.* Who doesn't love the feeling of marking things off a checklist? Booya! So, let's begin collecting items from our checklist of essential organizing tools.

Building Your Organizing Tool Kit

Everyone loves an adventurous scavenger hunt, right? It might be even more fun and challenging if you set a timer and work together to find what you need from the checklist below! I know with my boys that setting a timer turned any activity from being "a boring bummer" to "seriously savage" in a matter of seconds. If your kiddos get bored or need more time to hunt, then break for a snack or quick energy building activity. *Doing activities together is not about* the **race to finish,** *but more about the* **relationship built** *between each activity.*

1. **Banker Box**

    It is the classic sturdy cardboard box, historically used to store old tax files. It is easy on the back to lift, has side openings for handles, and has a lid to protect your items between organizing sessions. The homework table is not a viable substitute since that is where your child must work distraction-free. I have found that Office Depot/Office Max carries the best assortment of banker boxes for one bundled value price and can be assembled and flattened as needed. If not, any small-size box with a sturdy bottom, handles, and a lid will work, so little helpers can assist carrying it as well. Between organizing sessions, cover your kit with its lid to keep out the curious (babies, spouses, and pets alike). I like to put a sign on my box that says:

"No touching; you will be gravely harmed." Protecting your tool kit means you won't have to waste time with your child on another scavenger hunt and can begin working right away.

2. **Brother™ Label Maker**

   This $35 investment is non-negotiable for a gazillion and a half reasons. No further discussion required. The label maker has magical powers, people ... especially over the most stubborn, most distracted kids, who resist taking part in organizing anything. Out comes the label maker, and like a hypnotist, their mood takes a drastic turn. They will be excited to follow your every command. I recommend the Brother™ P-Touch Model: PT – 1890, which offers the best value for the money by including the label tape and batteries in its combo packaging.

   NOTE: The label maker's instructions can be funky to follow, so here is a quick recap from my first book as a snappy guide to give you a head start and save on excessive use of label tape.

Epic Organizing Adventure:
How to Make the Most Awesome Labels Ever!!!

Top 4 settings to adjust on your label maker:

1. **Font Tab** – Select "bold" so you can see labels during the day or at night when eyes get weary.

2. **Margin** – Select "narrow" to avoid wasting tape for each print-off.

3. **Label length** – Set for 3.5 instead of "max," which will adjust the font size to make it fit within your label range. The max setting causes the labels to be inconsistent and not professional looking.

4. **Underline/Frame** – All labels look best with a finished frame rather than with just a font that is floating on the surface the label is adhered to. "Hands" or "Candy" are kid fan favorite options. Print different fonts for your family members in a variety of frames to place on water bottles or other belongings while you learn... Enjoy the adventure!

3. The Basics

- 1 retractable contractor-style measuring tape
- 1 small hammer
- 10 nails of different sizes
- 1 clear shoe box with a lid. Clear is best so you can see all your organizing doodads inside, and you can easily grab what you need.

4. Office Supplies

Place the following items (that can fit) inside the clear shoe box:

- 1 clipboard with your favorite writing pen/pencil attached. Trust me, you will lose it a hundred times if it is not attached with ribbon or VELCRO®. Been there, done that, until I attached mine.

- 1 clipboard (or pocket folder) per family member to hold future tasks
- 10 binder clips
- 10 paper clips (jumbo preferred)
- 10 rubber bands
- 10 small adhesive mailing labels
- 10 large adhesive mailing labels
- 2 medium point permanent markers
- 1 handy hole puncher
- 1 seriously sharp scissors (for the parent)
- 1 easy-to-hold scissors (for the child)

5. **Kitchen Supplies**
   - 10 medium zipper style plastic bags
   - 10 large zipper style plastic bags
   - 1 roll of kitchen-sized garbage bags
   - 10 plastic handled grocery bags
   - 1 roll of blue painters' tape
   - 1 package of baby wipes to sanitize your items and the area as you work.

Build a Bin of Bins™ and Bag of Bags™ Boutique

If you didn't create your at-home boutique while reading the first book, then I highly suggest starting now! No time like the present, right?!? I consider this organizing concept just as essential as the Organizer Tool Kit: A Boutique of both Bins and Bags.

I place all types of misfit zipper pouches or clear zippered bags (the type that sheet sets are sold in) inside the largest of those types of bags, creating what I call a Bags of Bags Boutique™. I repeat the concept with bins, by creating a Bin of Bins Boutique™ inside one 18-gallon lidded tote. I include anything from misfit food containers (with or without lids) to hearty phone boxes or inserts that can be used to organize contents inside a drawer. Having this boutique available to me 24/7 allows me to get to the finish line faster. AND, by repurposing what I already have on hand, I get bottom-line savings. Involve your kiddo to help label your boutiques. They can assist in delivering items to them on your behalf, get familiar with the contents, and find what they need for upcoming projects.

Way to prove your Team is ready to take down *any* clutter on *any* given day!

 You have successfully built your Organizing Tool Kit and earned your first stack of clutter-free coins to keep your organizing game strategy strong if you successfully completed the following:

❏ Bought a Brother label maker and stocked it with batteries…YES!
❏ Know the basics of working the label maker – set the font, label length, and printing a variety of decorative frames.

- ❏ Stocked the remaining in your Organizing Tool Kit and checked it – TWICE!
- ❏ Marked "Do not touch or you will be harmed" on your tool kit to protect its contents at all costs.
- ❏ You already feel that your team is starting a winning streak by building your tool kit.
- ❏ You have created a reasonably-sized inventory of Bins and Bags in your Boutique.

By completing this chapter, I know you both totally got this organizing jam allllll going on. Maybe you're not feeling as confident in each other's skills, or maybe accomplishing these tasks together was much harder than you thought (since each person has their own ideas to communicate). These are ALL great things to talk about and decide who shall be the lead on which tasks. Maybe the parent finds the items and the child cleans, counts and checks it off the list before placing it in the tool kit or vice versa? There is no right or wrong way…it is *your* home, *your* ideas, *your* unique family's Organizing Tool Kit. If further motivation and enthusiasm is lacking from either party, let the creative vibes run wild and decorate your kit using Sharpies®, stickers, or colorful duct tape. Overall, you will realize how much fun organizing can be when accomplished together…snap a pic to capture this milestone moment!

MATTERS
— OF THE —
MIND

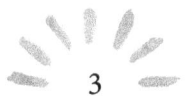

3

WHEN A MASTER GATEKEEPER TRAINS A DOMAIN DEFENDER

Your family home is your sanctuary from the bustling outside world. Your child's room is equally sacred. Typically, these spaces are the only place where you both can retreat. You could pay for an all-inclusive, 5-star resort stay for your family, offering room service, laundry care, and daily housekeeping. But eventually, you will need to return to work to pay for it all. Your home is designed to be a place where all members of your family can refresh their spirit, renew their energy, and reflect on their work and school days. When your space is organized, it brings calmness out of the chaos of your everyday life as a family.

You already learned how to become a Master Gatekeeper in my first book; however, here's a quick definition recap:

One who has strong awareness and understanding that, as the Master Gatekeeper, they "hold the key" to deciding *what* objects are *granted* access to their home. A Master Gatekeeper would not randomly offer hundreds of keys to hundreds of earthly humans (or creepy aliens), allowing access to their home. No. They must be cordially invited.

This concept applies to *all* items, including future clutter. A Gatekeeper Parent and their Domain Defender Kiddo have the POWER to decide *what* has access the home—from excessive bulk food purchases, random receipts, kids' doodads, and online shopping items, just to name a few. A Master Gatekeeper understands the true power they now have as a parent and will raise up their kiddos with that same mindset, helping them become *Domain Defenders* (my boys get full credit for this title because, "Mom, it sounds wayyy cooler for kids" works for me!). Domain Defenders know it requires being *alert* and *aware* and exerting daily *self-control* to decide *what* is granted access to their home, room, and backpack. These defenders are *power-full* not *power-less* … muscle-flex moment please!

I want to share a common story from a client's perspective.

Domain Defending was a challenging concept for our client's daughter Claire, an avid artist and lover of all things crafty. Creative Claire's bedroom had begun bursting at the seams with her art. Her mom asked Wurth Organizing to transform the space that had become a catchall for everything Claire had crafted over the years. Her mom wanted Claire to have a space to create once again, but her projects and supplies had gotten out of hand. We all loved the idea and couldn't wait to help her kick this project into action. I asked her how much time (between dance practice and school) she could devote each week to her craft projects. Claire wanted to start out with a goal of one completed project each weekend, whether it be beading a bracelet or freehand coloring.

We set out to gather all her craft and art supplies together in one location—everything from markers, twistable crayons, wooden pencils, and watercolors to stamp and sticker projects, loom kits, and boxes of beads. Our team stood back in silence and waited for Claire and her mom's response after seeing stacks of craft kits and baskets of different supplies all together in one place and completely covering her desk. Her mom said, "Wow, Claire. I didn't realize you had acquired so many different types of craft supplies."

The disconnect stemmed from Claire and her mom not yet developing their Gatekeeping/Defending skills. Often when they were out shopping, Claire would beg her mom for something new for her to craft because she "needed it." When Christmas and birthdays would roll around, she kept getting more and more.

The solution for Claire and her mom was to take some of her excess supplies to their local Boys & Girls Club so other kids in the neighborhood could enjoy working on projects of their own after school. Creative Claire went from overloaded to refreshed about the projects she would tackle next in her newly-organized crafting space.

If Claire and her mom had been taught about Gatekeeping, they would have spent *less time collecting* and could have dedicated *more quality time* finishing projects together that were started and forgotten.

Domain Defender Training

The reason every household needs at least one Gatekeeper Parent is that once clutter enters your home, someone has to decide whether to use it, hang it, share it, post it, maintain it, clean it, file it, discard it, donate it, or trash it. Phew! Making decisions about all the items flowing into your home almost sounds like another full-time job. Most kids and adults would say, "No way! I am not interested in accepting this new position. It is too much work, and I would rather do something wayyy more fun!"

When no one is making these decisions, clutter builds and invades our domains. We must plan for a full-on attack:

- ✓ The initial step toward being a Master Gatekeeper Parent is recognizing a *decision* must be made about every item that enters your family's home.
- ✓ It's best to make that decision *before* you or your child consider acquiring an item or to assist your Domain Defender child right *after* it has entered your home.
- ✓ The *more* your child can *protect* from a home invasion, the *less* clutter there will be to *deflect* as a Domain Defender.
- ✓ This means turning *off* the "I will deal with it *someday*" setting and turning *on* the "I will deal with it *now*" setting.

A good example is when your child comes home from a birthday party with a goodie bag full of knick-knack toys and candy treats. Instead of letting that bag find even a temporary home in your child's room, go through the bag with them upon arriving home. You can ask your child to line up all the items, from their *least* favorite to their *most* favorite. For the least favorite items, ask if they would like other kids to enjoy playing (or eating) those items, since they don't need them. If so, they can share them with another family member or friend and place them in a marked bag. Explain the double bonus—since they are a true Domain Defender, they will not have to find a place to store them.

If your child wants to keep it all, then as a Defender, they must provide three unique reasons *why* for each item. This engages them to unleash their executive functioning brain skills, which are required for quality decision-making. Today, it's decisions regarding their goodie bag. Tomorrow, it's decisions about quality books to read or healthy food selections when you are not present. No matter what the situation or circumstance, you can help your child defend the family domain by learning to make quick decisions on what is being granted access to your home and what needs tossed, recycled, or donated—from bouncy balls they got at the haircut place, to coloring pages from the restaurant kids' menus.

If you don't regularly use something in your daily life, it is clutter. Period. No exception. No further reasoning nor negotiating required. It must serve a true, consistent purpose in our life. Otherwise, it can serve another better.

Here's a scenario that demonstrates the effectiveness of mastering gatekeeping for your home: You head to your local superstore to pick up a few last-minute grocery items. The dollar section is conveniently placed smack in the front, where the carts are as you enter. Coincidence? Ha … I think NOT! Of course, your child's curiosity (and maybe yours) is on high alert after seeing the colorful bins of the latest goodies on display.

You know you don't need another darling magnet shopping list and pen set for your fridge, but this one has a super cute saying on it, and your kiddo likes the glow-in-the-dark-sparkle pen that comes with it. They're only a dollar you tell yourself, and you toss them and a few extras (why not?) into your shopping cart. You pay for it at checkout and shove the receipt somewhere in your bag or pocket. Upon returning home, the bag is plopped on top of the kitchen table or shoved in an open cupboard, with the other inventory you already have at home. You don't want to deal with it *now.* You will address it *someday* later, along with the other 1,000 "laters" of inventory in multiple locations (since they have yet to be properly organized and stored … LATER).

Now … Let's compare to how a Master Gatekeeper Parent with their Domain Defending Child would handle the situation:

Child: These gel pen sets are epic! These have all the colors I love. So can you buy it for me?

Parent: These pen sets are sooo fun to look at, and I appreciate all the unique things they have on sale, but we don't *need* to buy any of these items today.

Child: Please, please, please … I want it. It's super cool and sparkling. And it's all my favorite colors.

If your child begs over and over and over again to buy the item, then here are some negotiating options to offer:

Parent: When would you use this sparkle pen and pad set? You don't use the set you have at home, which is even nicer than this one. If you really want an extra set for when you go to grandma's house, then you can use some of your allowance or birthday money to buy it. I will offer to pay for half and then *you* can pay for the other half with that money. How does that sound?

Child: Ummm, I don't know what I want to do.

Parent: Okay, how about you carefully hold onto the sparkle pen set in the cart while we shop, and we can talk about it again *before* we cross the finish line at checkout. Sounds like a good plan?

Child: Yes, good plan!

Parent: Okay, here we are at checkout. What do you want to do? How about I take a picture of that item and its bar code as a reminder? If you still want the item later, we can order it online or request it as future gift … Deal?

Child: It's a deal!

If the child truly wants to buy the pen set that very day, then confirm the deal you offered (you pay half, and they pay half with their allowance or birthday monies). Be sure to collect on their debt before the product is handed over! This is also a two-fold teaching example—both a gatekeeping lesson and an illustration about what to remember when doing "deals" with people in real life.

If the child already has too many new sets at home but likes this one even more, the above domain defending rules apply—they must either donate or re-gift any unopened sets. This enforces gatekeeping and healthy decision-making instead of supporting a consumerist and wasteful mentality.

When the transaction is complete, the cashier hands over the receipt and some coupons. The experienced Master Gatekeeper Parent and Domain Defender Child step aside from the counter and do the following:

- ❏ Glance through the coupons to see if they really, really, really need to buy any of those items before the coupons expire.
- ❏ If certain coupons are not needed, the child sees their wise parent hand the coupons back to the cashier, saying, "Please pass these along to another customer. Thank you."
- ❏ This may result in a confused look from the cashier, but good gatekeepers get over the odd glares quickly.
- ❏ As the child gets older, the parent can ask the child to hand it back to the cashier on their behalf.
- ❏ As for the receipt, the trained Gatekeeper Parent either circles the credit card type, date, and total amount for future bookkeeping, or they can ask their child to circle these for them, so they can learn by doing.
- ❏ Done … done … and done!
- ❏ Lastly, the trained Gatekeeper Parent leaves the store with a stellar smile, and while driving home, reviews with their Domain Defender Child their experience and all the tiny but important decisions that were made.
- ❏ Upon arriving home, the child assists in either putting away their recent purchases or returning the canvas errands bag to its designated location.

Dang, that's good! By doing 10 seconds of Master Gatekeeping at the store, you will get into the healthy habit of making quicker decisions while avoiding being sucked into the "we will deal with it later cycle." Later usually joins forces with other "later friends" left in your car, your home, your kiddo's closet, and elsewhere in your life.

Later often morphs into "much later" before eventually transforming into "never." The sooner you grasp the "Now is better than later" concept, the sooner you gain control of your home and your child's room, and you can banish all those invaders of your home for good.

One-Minute Rule™

This concept was taught in the first book, but here's a recap of its definition: If a task can be done in one minute or under, then it's something you need to do immediately.

When decisions become repeatedly delayed, belongings continue to build, layer upon layer. Ultimately, this accumulation makes it even more difficult to catch up. You are a smart person and so, likely, is your child. Whether they are emotionally challenged or physically challenged, whether they are 3 years old or 13 years old, I believe, in my heart, that you and your child—and every single person on this planet—are capable of making simple solution-oriented decisions and placing things where they belong.

If preschoolers can place their belongings in a classroom cubby, then surely, with your guidance, your child can put away their things at home as well, too. Shocking…right? You can help them make small changes in their daily routine that eventually transform into habits. When something needs to be done, the first question to ask should be, "Is a task required?" If the answer is yes, then you and your child are the decision-makers. If the task can be accomplished now, encourage them to do it. Right then! If the task is not done, it will lead to 1,000 laters. I will get to that later, and that later, and etc. However, if a task requires more than one minute, recognize that task is a project and discuss the best location for it to be placed and completed later—maybe on their designated homework table or on their desk with other more complex projects.

Playful Habit Practices ..."Negotiate to Motivate" ™

Whenever you can turn practice of a new habit into something playful, it will increase kids' interest ten-fold. Doing simple tasks repeatedly helps to form them into consistent habits—from putting their toothbrush back in the drawer, stashing their pajama set under their pillow, and making their bed to the best of their age and ability…all are importance tasks that can become habits over time with practice.

I also LOVE to *"Negotiate to Motivate"* my boys when required! Oliver would do anything for salty snacks in his lunch, while Devon could be easily lured with sweets treats. I got tired of the ranting reminders each morning, so I would set a 7-minute timer and state what tasks the boys were required to complete "in the back of the house" before the timer went off (e.g., make their bed, get dressed, brush teeth, and gel hair). The boys needed to *"report for duty"* in the hallway, fully dressed for the school day. I have no military background but LOVE making the everyday bore into something more. It was not only hilariously fun to see them dashing around as the timer ticked by, but it made tasks an interactive game rather than a boring job. If one child was ahead of schedule, we encouraged that warrior brother to support his fellow comrade when, needed.

Playful practices like these offer many skills and experiences ... it truly is endless and eye-opening for EVERYONE! Consequences for goofing off were also explained prior the start of the timer. These might include an extra chore after school or loss of lunch treats, allowance money, or game time.

Epic Organizing Adventure:
Review and Redirect Behaviors

Read the above "Negotiate to Motivate" paragraph story together.

1. Discuss your family's Top 3 daily challenges and talk about possible solutions where you could "Negotiate to Motivate".

   _____
   _____
   _____

2. What fun activity could you do together when one needs to "Report for Duty"?

   _____

3. What would some consequences be if it doesn't happen?

   _____

I often would have the boys repeat the "game plan" back to me, so I knew it was clearly understood. We will cover more on discipline and consequences when we talk about my R.O.C.K. method in a later chapter.

You have created a Domain Defender when your child has learned to make daily *decisions* to *protect* their domain. By *rewarding* these behaviors, you will reinforce the building blocks for essential *life* and *relationship skills*. Initially, you may need to work alongside your child until they become a more independent and confident warrior, but this is what Master Gatekeeper Parents must do—teach, teach, teach! If you need to give each Defender their own unique title, then do so ... whatever it takes!

You have become a Master Gatekeeping Parent and a Domain Defending Child and earned another stack of clutter-free coins to keep your organizing game strategy strong if you successfully completed the following:

- ❏ Understood the role and responsibility of a Master Gatekeeping Parent and a Domain Defending Child.
- ❏ Discussed together the importance of recognizing a *decision* must be made about *every* item that enters your family's home.
- ❏ Together, you have conquered at least 5 scenarios dealing with items *after* they entered your home.
- ❏ Together, you have conquered at least 5 scenarios on items *before* they entered the home, such as things from work, school, hobby, or sports activities.
- ❏ Together, you have conquered 20 do-it-now-versus-later decisions: 10 for the parent and 10 for the child.
- ❏ You've shopped in at least 10 stores with your child and left with only the absolutely necessary items you

both truly needed (whether that was food, clothing, or toys).
- ❏ You have politely said "No" to cashiers, salespeople, or other service folks when offered coupons or marketing materials that you know neither of you will use.
- ❏ You and your child have consistently been discarding trash as quickly as possible from your purse/satchel/backpack and car.
- ❏ You and your child can tag-team to demonstrate the one-minute rule by making it a game and challenging each other.
- ❏ You have discussed and/or attempted some *playful practices* to help make forming new habits more interactive (so decision-making skills can be developed sooner rather than later).
- ❏ You have discussed and/or implemented some *consequences* to enforce the forming of these new habits.
- ❏ You have experienced at least 5 "Negotiate to Motivate" Epic Adventures to kick-start the new habit-forming process.

Congratulations! You are officially designated a Master Gatekeeper Parent and your child, an ultimate Domain Defender, who protects their family home from unwelcomed intruders of clutter. You're now ready to move on to become a Master Decision-Making Duo.

4

BECOME A MASTER DECISION-MAKING DUO

Did you know that the human brain develops from the back to the front? Therefore, the last place to develop is the prefrontal cortex area of the frontal lobe. This is where executive functioning skills come from—organizing skills, the ability to complete multistep projects, and effective decision-making!

The prefrontal cortex isn't fully developed during normal development until age 26 and not until age 32 in gifted individuals. This means you have ample time to establish concrete decision-making skills—skills that will be beneficial to your child for life! These facts further enforced my desire to truly ignite the organizer in **my** child!

Now that you and your child have mastered Gatekeeping/Domain Defending, I believe in my heart—100,000 percent—that you and your kiddo can and will become a Master Decision-Making Duo. This is not a complicated concept. It simply takes daily practice and consistent repetition until it becomes natural. We discussed this in depth in the *Ignite the Organizer in You* book, and the same holds true for kiddo-related decision-making. By working together, you both can DOMINATE!

During most organizing sessions, clients confess to me the following recurring statement: "I am just so disorganized (or my child is, or both of us are disorganized). I/we just can't get it together. There are piles of things everywhere."

I could record this phrase, and future clients could save energy by hitting the replay button rather than repeating the same frustrations. I empathize with them because their family situation is common, and they are not alone in feeling overwhelmed, feeling guilty, or feeling like a "bad" mom or dad. Once they understand my psychology-based approach toward creating organized systems for their home, hope blossoms.

One of our clients, Jolie, came to us after years of frustration. Her organizing personality was a Chaotic Combo of a Fast-Moving Train and a Container-a-holic. This was reflected in her child's personality—who was a Clock Chaser and a Methodical Mind. Their family life was so busy, she couldn't slow down to get organized, but she kept buying organizing items, which would collect dust in her garage, while she hoped to eventually make use of them. Jolie and her kiddoes were exhausted, overwhelmed, and didn't know where to start. She said, "I don't know where things are, and I don't know my schedule for today nor tomorrow. I don't like that I am not being the best example to my kids either."

Your Life's Layer Cake

At Wurth Organizing, we compare clutter in the home to a delicate layer cake. The clutter represents many sweet layers of life's activities and experiences. Some layers were created over months, while others span a few years. And some perhaps even decades. Eventually, this delicate layer cake becomes too tall, too heavy and splits, leaving a crumbling mess. Everyone's layer cake is unique to their life's minutiae. Having layers of life that surround you does not always mean you're disorganized; it simply means it is time to become a Master Decision-Maker. That's it. You can stop beating yourself up in the boxing ring over what you have been calling disorganization and put your energy into knocking out clutter with some heavy-hitting decision-making.

We told Jolie that her motivation to change their family dynamic and openness to learning new organizing skills is all that is required for success. By merely connecting with me, the rest is just stuff that needs to be dealt with through our future, ongoing sessions together.

It can be emotionally difficult for any parent to embrace their current situation, put aside their pride, stare straight into their cluttered piles of shame, and then bravely dial our number. But, right after making that call, hope begins. After our first session, Jolie told us, "I feel so much better already, just getting it off my chest and just talking about all this." Now *you* can take the next step on the journey, just like Jolie did.

Time to pump your fist in the air and watch the volume of things coming into your home gradually dwindle.

Epic Organizing Adventure: Decision-Making Domination

Now, we're going to take those skills and combine them to practice making decisions such as sorting through the schoolwork and flyers in your child's Friday Folder.

Speak out loud as you separate papers into 4 piles: need to toss, need to read/review (one for child, one for parent), and need to save.

- ❏ Have your child write the title of each pile on a separate piece of paper as a guide to encourage their engagement.
- ❏ Slide title pages into clear protective sleeves for future use or clip cover sheet to individual clipboards (the ones you got for your Organizing Tool Kit). The Paperwork Virus™ can't spread when clipped down, and this makes for easy surface cleaning with your kiddo's help.
- ❏ You kick-start the process, then alternate decision making.
- ❏ Remember, you can "Negotiate to Motivate" by stating that once you are done, there will be a snack, treat, or playtime.
- ❏ Once they are a seasoned Decision-Maker, your child will be able to tackle this process from start to finish—on their own ... such a glorious victory!

Below are common themes and suggested solutions:

Artwork/Schoolwork. Lay it all out and ask them what their absolute top three favorite items are and have them provide three unique reasons *why* for each item. If they can't give three different reasons, then it doesn't "make the cut to keep it," and the question is answered!

Awards. If they carry special value to you and/or your child, then slide them into a clear protective sleeve. Then have your child place them in a 3-inch-wide upright magazine tote for a future memory binder book or immediately clip up in their designated art gallery area, which we will address in the Kids' Rooms chapter.

Birthday party invitations. Take a quick glance at your calendar and the events that surround that date.

- For Automatic No or Yes: RSVP right then. If attending, mark it on the calendar and post a reminder 2 weeks before to purchase a gift.

- <u>For Maybe</u>: Will you and your child be on overload if they attend? Better to RSVP with "maybe" and state you are awaiting confirmation on other scheduled events that may conflict. Out of respect for the host, a "maybe" response is better than "zero" response while you are deciding.

Discount offers. Only save ones you will use. File them in alpha order in a retro recipe box and place in the car console.

Future events. Your child will not be able to participate in all events. If further time is required, clip flyer on the spouse/family clipboard to discuss perhaps a Sunday night, before the start of the week.

Future homework or test info. Put any assignments that need to be completed in their homework space.

Graded homework or tests. Attach to their clipboard rather than creating a random pile with no purpose. You can then review what concepts they understood and what needs improvement.

Large Scale/3D Projects. Upon completion of the project, take a picture of your child holding it, so the memory is captured before it leaves for school. You can also make a short video of them describing their project, what they learned, and its importance to them. Email the image to yourself, print it, and place it in a protective sleeve to keep for a future memory book or hang it in their art gallery. You both will feel confident the memory was captured and this method also serves as a back-up option if the project gets accidentally ruined while on its way to the classroom.

School field trip info. Complete the form, attach payment, return to the child, and mark it on the calendar. As they get older, have them complete the form and you review/sign it.

Thank you cards. Quickly read the card with your child and toss if it serves no purpose. If a sweet memory is attached, then place it in your child's memory box/book.

Organizing is a constant process of *reaction* and *adjustment* to activities experienced in daily life. Every decision avoided has consequences that eventually cause confusion—day after day, layer upon layer. Awareness of your decisions is the flaming core of your organizing process, and that flame must burn strongly and not fizzle.

In the beginning of your parent/child organizing process, you will experience a few rounds of volume reduction. You will make multiple quality decisions and, as a result, you will reduce the overall volume around you. Success in this effort sets you up to make even more and quicker decisions. Round and round and round you will go until you reach your final decision-making round for a particular space ... and boy, does it feel and look AMAZING to be there!

You have become a Decision-Making Duo and earned another stack of clutter-free coins to keep your organizing game strategy strong if you successfully completed the following:

- ❏ You and your child *caught* yourselves making good decisions or recognize when you were *not* making them. It is the awareness of the activity (or lack thereof) that matters most.
- ❏ You both passed on keeping any unnecessary school papers, vendor promotional flyers, cards, or invites unless there was a serious interest, or they had sentimental value.
- ❏ You passed on excessively adding to your Things to Read/Review pile and are pleased with the current amount of reading inventory.

- ❏ Together, you and your child powered through a typical batch of schoolwork, art, and flyers, dividing decisions into three decision-making piles: Need to Toss, Need to Read and Review, and Need to Save.
- ❏ Your child has independently powered through a typical batch of schoolwork, art, and flyers and successfully decided how to divide into the three decision-making piles.
- ❏ You have taken a picture or video of your child holding large or 3D Projects before they leave your home for future memory keeping.
- ❏ You have discussed with your child future solutions to store their schoolwork and artwork for items they cherish most.

Way to dominate the days! Now you are ready to seriously start "kicking ace" and master the terrific Top 4 A's of the Organizing Game in the next chapter.

5

KICKING ACE: MASTERING THE FOUR A'S OF ORGANIZING TOGETHER

Please refer to the 4 A's chapter in the *Ignite the Organizer in You* book so you and your child understand the correct order of the 4 A's of Organizing: Assess, Attack, Assign and Accountable. The order is important to make sure you can confidently move forward and not "Hit, Run, Strike Out," as discussed in the baseball scenario. Here's a quick snapshot to refresh your memory about the sequence from first base through the home run:

- **Assess** the space and its function.
- **Attack** by separating items into four piles–keep, consign, donate, and maybe.
- **Assign** an organized system; learn and use my P.O.P. Method™ when selecting completion products.
- **Accountable** to yourself, your family, and your home to complete and maintain one space at a time.

In a moment, I will share the scenario of me sorting through my son Oliver's super sacred rock collection (true story folks!)

to show you how we practice the 4 A's of organizing together. But first, I'll explain each phase and the mindful method behind each one.

Assess Phase

I would suggest handling this phase alone, so you can save your energy for later, when you'll need to focus on all that is required to transition the volume/challenging space (or collection) into a well-organized solution. When you're ready, you can review some ideas with your child, so they feel involved and will be more likely to take ownership and interest when you move to the next phase. Most importantly, I want to highlight what is involved in the **Attack Phase** when working with your child.

Attack Phase

We have found that the best way to kick off the Attack Phase with our clients' children is to **help them define their top three favorites of whatever theme we are working on, whether it is toy sets or collections.** I ask them to give me three solid reasons why they love each set, such as "It's fun to build," or "It's challenging, and I feel good once my project is complete." Then, I discuss how fortunate they are to own these three toys sets because some kids don't own any sets, and many have very few toys at all.

I discuss how they would feel if they didn't own any fun toy sets. Usually, they understand my reasoning and are sympathetic to the conditions of other children in their community. I then ask them which sets of toys they think they have enjoyed and would like to pass along, so other children can begin enjoying them. They must be confident in their decision-making and not become emotionally or mentally confused. Otherwise, their doubtful mind will shut down like a steel door to Batman's private cave.

When it comes to the Attack Phase, *any* item decided upon has a great value lesson behind it. It MUST be acknowledged and encouraged, from a random plastic trinket from a past birthday party to a stuffed animal or video game. The important thing is to get them to start *making* decisions and *mentally* prioritizing. You wouldn't be short-tempered at your tumbling toddler, screaming, "Why can't you walk? What is the big deal? Why can't you get your act together already and do something?" Heck no! So, we need to visualize that, to our kiddo's brain, *"trying to make-a-decision"* is like learning to walk. They are mentally taking one small, struggling step at a time. They will stumble, then will fall. That is part of the *"learning to walk"* decision-making process in the Attack Phase. **Do not rob your child of this important phase experience. You would inevitably be delaying their brain development. Delaying their decision-making = delaying your child's overall development.**

Assign Phase

The focus of this phase is to Assign an organizing system to only the item that are being kept, therefore require a storage solution. A solution can be something as basic and boring as an old shoe box, shipping box, random containers or misfit styled baskets. ***The product and style of any solution can always be upgraded later…creating, assigning, labeling and implementing a new organizing system into one's lifestyle is what matters most.***

Check your perfectionist mind set at the door and make the progress happen by assigning solutions to all themes in the space.

Epic Organizing Adventure: Toy Virus Take Down

Before you attack and dissect what you are keeping, tossing, donating, or consigning, grab four cardboard boxes or plastic totes/tubs you have on hand. Then, hunt down your killer Organizing Tool Kit and decide who will label each box as follows:

Trash: For food trash, wrappers, broken items, you name it. It's pure trash.

Recycle: For items you can place in your own recycling bins or take to a recycling center.

Donate: Limit your recipients to no more than two. If the volume is large and time is limited, select a company that offers pick-up service. I believe all your items have value. Do you? However, every item doesn't keep the same value to you throughout your child's entire life.

Consignment/Gift: You have packed and unpacked the same toy set repeatedly, and your child still shows no interest in playing with it. Better to bring a smile to another child in your community this very week! By making the decision to pass that item on, you are giving a gift to someone else. Consider starting an account in your child's name to encourage the giving spirit.

Maybe Pile of Misfits: Remember my reference to this in my first book? Just like the Island of Misfit Toys in the classic movie *Rudolph the Red-Nosed Reindeer*, there are items we are not sure what to do with, or who to pass them along to. If they are unsure, ask them to explain three reasons *why* it could be a keeper and ask them their reasons for being unsure about letting it go. Usually, they can only provide one or two valid reasons. It is more difficult to think of three reasons (which is why we set three as the magic number).

NOTE: Most kiddos (and most adults, too) have never paused to think about *why* they desire to keep an item. Thinking about these reasons helps *everyone* mentally map what the item might mean to them or why it might be better to give to another.

ALTERNATIVE OPTIONS: If you or your child are really struggling about letting an item go directly to the donate box, even if they no longer use it regularly, there are some alternatives to donating:

1. Place the item in their personal memory bin.
2. Snap a pic of your child with the item, save it on your camera roll, and donate the item.
3. Snap a pic, print the image and place it in a protective sleeve to store for a future memory bin or binder book, and donate memory item.
4. Repurpose the item. For example, a souvenir cup from a ball game can hold a child's coin collection.

Negotiating the Attack and Assign Phases

Mommy: Oliver, you have gathered so many interesting rocks this past year. Tell me which ones are your absolute favorites.

Oliver: All of them.

Mommy: Well, I am sure you do love all of them. But if you had to show me your top three most favorite, which ones would those be?

Oliver: This one is my most favorite because it has these cool swirl marks all over it. Oh, and I love this one because it has these sparkles and stripes. Annndddd this one because it's the biggest.

Mommy: I see you have collected so many types. But we can't store them all on your closet shelf because we need to make room for other collections you also want to keep on that shelf. We don't want your collections to feel all smashed together either. They need room and space around them.

Oliver, do you think it would be super cool if we use this big glass pickle jar to protect your rocks? We can clean it out right now, be good recyclers of the environment by repurposing it AND you'll be able to see all the sides of your rocks whenever you want?

Oliver: Yes. I like that idea.

Mommy: Okay, so put those top three most favorite rocks in now. What about these others? Are there others that are special to you? If so, then you need to tell me three unique reasons why certain ones are special enough to be placed in the jar.

Brain muscle moment: The purpose of this exercise is to get Oliver to really *engage in the action of decision-making* and to understand himself better, as well as his reasons for wanting to keep or pass on items. The more in tune he is with his needs, wants, desires, and the logic (or lack of logic) behind his ownership decisions, the more confident he will become in himself.

This skill will transfer to his homework, team sports involvement, and eventually his choice in peer group. The list of experiences will grow as his brain continues to develop. The prefrontal cortex of the brain is where organizing, decision-making, and executive functioning skills originate. Brain power flexing, one, two, three reps… we are working it!

Now, back to Oliver.

Oliver: I like this rock because of the purple colors, but don't really like anything else about it. I guess I don't need to keep this one. It can go back in the garden to be with the other rocks and flowers …

We continue to sort through the remainder of his rocks. Once the jar is filled to the top with Oliver's favorite collection, a few stragglers remain. He now must decide what to swap out of the jar if he desires to place something new in. We agree that the unselected rocks still have value to the backyard, so that's where they will go.

We will not create another collection jar unless he decides to give up that prime shelf space the rock collection is using. Basically, he is learning that he *can't* have it all, all the time. However, he *can* have his most favorite rocks on display and rotate those choices in the collection jar any time he wants.

Oliver: I want to label my jar using the label maker!

Mommy: Great idea! Let's do it and take a selfie to show Daddy at dinner so he can see what we worked on today. High fives for us!!!

Boundaries are a beautiful thing. They teach *self-control* and *discernment*. They also teach how to fine-tune *appreciation, respect,* and *stewardship* for one's items versus hoarding inventory and wasting its value. Boundaries also prevent us from falling into the mentality of "having more makes me feel better."

This cycle can start with a jar of rocks as a child, but trust me folks, it can easily lead to closets full of clothes and jammed garage bays upon adulthood. This is why the final phase, **Accountable**, becomes even more important. It creates built-in boundaries to help guide you, which we will discuss in more detail in the Kids' Rooms chapter. This leads me right into the merry maintenance mode in the Accountable Phase, which I call the sweet spot.

Accountable Phase

Sunday night, after family dinner, Phil announces it is time for everyone to tidy up the house. This means we each walk around to pick up and put back an arsenal of items—drink cups to the sink, gum wrappers to the trash, and dirty laundry placed in the hamper.

After a full weekend of soccer game outings, things at home can easily unravel everywhere and for everyone. Sunday night is the perfect night to put it all back, so you can start out strong on Monday, prepared for the busy week ahead. It doesn't matter which item belongs to which family member. We are a family and lift one another up as a family. In the kitchen chapter, I will dive in further about how we are all involved on Sunday night—from meal planning, food shopping and putting it all away, to prepping lunches and snacks for the coming week.

You aced the 4 A's of Organizing and earned another stack of clutter-free coins to keep your organizing game strategy strong if you successfully completed the following:

Assess Phase

❏ You privately assessed a variety of your child's toy sets or collections to see what works and what doesn't in regard to purpose and organizing.

Attack Phase

❏ Together, you selected a toy set or themed collection (such as a rock collection) to work on together in the Attack and Assign Phases.
❏ You patiently listened to your child's needs and desires about their collections, and together, you devised a plan to reduce the collection and chose what product will be used to store the final inventory.
❏ You understand that they are "learning to walk," making quality decisions as their brain develops.
❏ You attacked all the inventory of the collection, deciding what to keep, toss, donate, consign/gift, or place in a maybe pile.
❏ The Maybe Pile of Misfits has been reviewed. Either all items have been relocated, you've agreed to review the pile at another point in time, or you've discussed some creative "alternative options."

Assign Phase

❑ A final organizing system for a variety of themes has been discussed or assigned with a label and celebration hugs are underway.

Accountable Phase

❑ You and your child have selected a day for tidying up, so you stay accountable to whatever organizing systems and rhythms you have created as a family.

Who is ready to be empowered? That is what the next chapter is allll about. To this day, it is still one of my most favorite concepts to teach, since this is where the most dramatic changes begin to develop in family member relationships.

6

EMPOWER YOUR CHILDREN, NOT ENABLE THEM™

**Train up a child in the way he should go,
and when he is old, he will not depart from it.**

– Proverbs 22:6, KJV

I first learned this poignant Proverb during a Mothers of Preschoolers (MOPS) meeting at my home church, Scottsdale Bible Church. When my first child, Devon, was born, I took on the role of a mother. I not only filled his heart with love and his belly with nutrients— but equally important—I filled his mind with essential life skills. I view our home as life's classroom, where Phil and I are the teachers, providing innovative life lessons for Devon and Oliver each day.

This includes everything from our foundation in our faith to household responsibilities, from character building to respect for our belongings and kindness for people in our community. These survival skills go into their "life backpack" so that they can embark on their journey into adulthood feeling prepared and independent.

This is how my hubby and I see our role as parents. We are intentionally committed to this job, every day, until our kiddos leave our loving family nest. Whether you are a parent, grandparent, or caregiver, it is your responsibility to train up and provide the children you care for with an arsenal of essential life skills to use as they grow into adulthood. Their life backpack will be well-stocked with skills needed to handle a multitude of life's blessings and challenges.

Organizing Skills Needed to Survive in the Wild World

Over the years I have found that when I explained new teaching concepts to parents and kiddos, they were able to understand the concepts more easily if a visual icon or storyline analogy was provided to represent it. Since *"organizing skills are life skills"*™, it seemed naturally fitting to use outdoor, adventure themed icons to represent the wild world around us. These are the *life skills* required to learn, master, and thrive (not just survive) once we leave the family nest (campground) and venture onward and upward to fully experience all that life has to offer us in adulthood!

- **Compass** – To show them the way of faith-based knowledge and respectful stewarding of what they've been given.
- **Binoculars** – Attention to details of their work and their overall surroundings and safety.
- **Home Tent** – Love for your child and their respect for family members and others who support them until adulthood.

- **Map** – Understanding of time, time management, and how long activities and projects take to navigate and complete.
- **Notebook & Pencil** - Organizing skills and related responsibilities.
- **Rocky Mountain** – Resilience and self-control to handle the rocky roads ahead that will challenge them to reach new heights.
- **Rope of Connection** – Manners and interaction with others.
- **Water Bottle** – Healthy understanding of food and nutrition.

Using such skills affects many aspects of our children's daily lives, including keeping track of schoolwork, organizing their room, and ensuring toys and game pieces stay together. It is our responsibility to teach our children these important skills.

As parents, we draw upon the life skills our parents taught us, as well as our own natural-born abilities. Hopefully, you are fortunate enough to have learned from your family and to have further developed your own God-given basic skills. As you mature, you can reflect on these and further fine-tune your innate skills.

In this chapter, I am going to provide you with the building materials to help teach your children the skills that they will need to fill their life backpacks. You've already mastered gatekeeping and decision-making. This chapter will expand on those proficiencies with skills specific to helping your children thrive.

Compass

A device that is always correct and dependable in guiding you in the right direction, whether traveling alone or in a group. It is important to show them the way of faith-based knowledge and respectful stewarding of what they've been given.

From the very beginning, I have explained to the boys that everything we own comes from God. He blesses us with the money to purchase our belongings, and therefore, it is up to us to steward those items accordingly. Just like we would not throw the Bible on our dirty garage floor, it is not okay to lay their bikes and helmets on the floor instead of properly placing them back on the bike rack.

If they can't respect and steward what they are given, then it is removed. They must either earn it back with appropriate, respectful behavior, or it's time to discuss passing it along for another child to enjoy. No matter your faith or spiritual beliefs, all things have value and deserve care and respect. These are excellent truths to remember in all you do.

Binoculars

A handy instrument that allows the viewer to see things from far away, more up close and in finer detail.

It's sooo very important in life to always pay attention to detail. We remind our boys to look around their desk and on the field to "check their area" to see what items they may have left behind. We tell them to always, always double-check their work before handing it in for grading, and to never, ever assume anything. We advise them to confirm requirements for a project or repeat their understanding of the assignment back to the teacher.

Attention to detail in life is HUGE ... SO HUGE! Even the smallest of details, when missed, can yield a big impact for your child. You can support them—in school and life—by teaching them at an early age to be mindful of all details.

Epic Organizing Adventure: Increasing Attention to Detail

How do you spell x? I make the boys look up words in an old-school, hardback Webster's dictionary—not online. I don't give them the answer. They start the work themselves; I am nearby to assist if they get stuck, and they honestly like using the book! Have your child select any 5 words, and then require them to look them up. Then decide the next 5 words together and see who can find them faster...time yourselves and treasure the hunt of it all.

Homework. You can't scold them to do their homework if they don't understand the concept being taught, right? Devon would say, "Mommy, can you help me with my homework?" I would say, "Yes, I would love to! You work through the entire worksheet, then double-check that your work is correct. When you are finished, come get me for the questions you completely do not understand. You do your part first, and Mommy can help you finish." This builds your child's confidence and empowers them to try difficult tasks first instead of enabling them to avoid hard work by doing the work for them.

Try this approach at least 5 times during the school week, check it off below and discuss what strategies work best.

_____ 1 _____ 2 _____ 3 _____ 4 _____ 5

There are many opportunities we have as parents to help empower our children to become independent and gain the life skills they need. Here are some additional examples:

 ## Home Tent

This protective shelter represents the love for your child and their respect for fellow family members and others who support them until adulthood.

Unconditional love, support, and encouragement are essential to raising a healthy, close-knit family. There are also endless chores and responsibilities required of everyone to make the home run smoothly.

The following are some helpful ways to increase a child's awareness and appreciation for their Home Tent:

- **Household duties.** Our sons help with putting dishes away, setting the table, putting away laundry and groceries, and keeping the house tidy. They literally know where everything belongs, in every single room—from batteries to Band-Aids. You make a mess? You clean it up or help another clean theirs … we are ALL in this together, living in one tent.

- **Team efforts.** When Daddy is running late to work or I'm late leaving for a speaking event, the boys know to jump in and help load our cars so we can quickly arrive at our next destination. When one child is running behind for a soccer game, then other knows to take action and help fill a water bottle. If there is any form of complaining, the consequence is doing double duty on tasks.

 **Map**

Knowing how to navigate through tasks and understanding accurate measurement of time and overall time management is mega huge life skill to master. When you understand how to navigate the map (tasks and time), then you will understand how to travel from Point A to Point B, from single night homework to multi-step projects.

This one life skill that is, tragically, forgotten to be taught yet can be the most impactful in a child's life. I feel children today are severely lacking in mastering this life skill all the way up until middle school. Yet their parents haven't mastered it themselves. How can they teach them when they, too, are running life on a never-ending treadmill? Want to know how to resolve that debacle? LEARN TOGETHER, TRAIN TOGETHER!

The day Devon missed his ride. So many teaching moments have occurred over the years. When Devon began third grade (at a new school, I might add), he was chronically late getting dressed in enough time to catch a ride with Daddy to school. After what we called "too many get out of jail free cards," Phil and I agreed it was empowerment time and what the consequence would be. The next time Devon wasn't ready, Phil drove off, leaving Devon screaming after him in the driveway, wearing only one shoe.

After the tears of disappointment stopped running down Devon's face and nerves were calmed, I sat with Devon at the desk in my office. I could have easily **enabled** him by driving him to school myself, but instead, I chose to **empower** him by outlining how he would spend his time at home that day.

He had to write a letter to his teacher about the choices he made that morning and what he plans to do differently in the future. In addition, he had to spend the hours of the school day completing his homework for the week and reading from his current library book. And there were no games nor TV for the remainder of the day.

I informed his teacher that morning of our empowerment decision. She wrote a note back commending us on our parenting approach and saying she respected us for doing that. Devon is now the first to get up and get ready. He then helps his younger brother get ready so they can leave for school on time. We did a similar empowerment lesson for Oliver, who was left behind when Daddy went to the gym one day without him. There have been plenty of mega meltdowns, with tears and snotty noses, but man, our boys know we mean what we say. They also know we are not trying to be mean parents. We are firm and loving and here to empower them, not enable them. It has helped them greatly to become more confident and successful students.

 ## Notebook & Pencil

This classic organizing duo represents core skills and related responsibilities that we need to keep track of every day. The earlier you can learn this life skill, the better prepared you will be as their parent and they will be as students in school and in life generally.

This book allows you to check the organizing life skill off in no time flat … Whoop! Whoop! But here are a few areas to fine-tune, allowing you and your child to not only survive, but truly thrive together! Here are some common battles and how to overcome them:

Epic Organizing Adventure: Let's Slay the Everyday!

Clean your room! How can they accomplish this if you don't invest the time into creating organized systems for them to follow in the first place, right? Help them to kick it off, and then circle back to see how they are progressing. If it is a constant frustration and dead end, pause to consider why. Maybe there isn't a system in place for certain themed items. When a system is developed, the likelihood of room cleaning success increases.

What themes did you both find that need solutions?

_____

Ready for inspection? I helped empower Devon (and not enable him) by setting some requirements for him. If he wanted to watch his favorite show or play games, he had to tidy up his room first. We made it fun by me asking him, "Ready for inspection?" If I found random things placed incorrectly, I would joke, saying something like, "Those aren't your shoes thrown in the corner instead of in your closet, right? I must be imagining your shoes over there ... Hmmm." I then acted surprised when he quickly put the shoes where they belonged. This still is a fun way to oversee accountability while my boys are learning organizing skills and putting their best efforts forward.

Try your own inspection approach 5 times this week, check it off below and discuss what strategies worked best.

_____ 1 _____ 2 _____ 3 _____ 4 _____ 5

Rocky Mountain

The rocky trails your child will travel will not always be smooth to walk, nor clearly marked. Teaching them to be resilient and embrace challenges as they are presented builds the strong inner confidence required for them to strive forward and not turn back without a solid effort. The same goes for our journey as their parents.

In year 10 of our marriage, we had our son Devon. He was a bright child from the start—walking at eight months (and we have the video to prove it) and easily bored with age-appropriate toys. So, we searched for activities to challenge him. He was always thinking, always moving, and always wanting to express himself. Everything was going along great until age three, when Devon became very vocal with his opinions. He would tell us to stop building his train sets. He would refuse to put away toys. He would disobey rules simply because we told him to do something. This Italian mama was perplexed and fresh out of discipline ideas.

A door for the defiant. Traditional time-outs were a joke. Devon would sit calmly in the corner, unaffected. I tried spanking with a pancake spatula, like my parents had done with me. Devon laughed out loud, saying, "That didn't hurt," while smiling in defiance. One day, a creative solution popped into my exhausted brain. It was an approach that I hoped would save our sanity and his safety.

At the time, we lived in a two-story home with stairs at every corner. I actually got the idea from the doors at Devon's preschool—they were Dutch style, with top and bottom halves that moved and locked independently of each another. We hired a handyman to cut his bedroom door in half, finishing the bottom half so that it was transformed into a Dutch door. We now had a solution for Devon's next moments of disaster.

The key was to narrow Devon's options. I could lock the bottom half of the door, keeping him safe, but leave the top open so I could peek on him when he was playing or napping. This gave Devon the independence he desperately craved, in a safe environment. And I was able to keep my sanity.

Devon and I are very similar creatures. We both take pleasure in overseeing processes and projects. We both know what we want and what we don't, and neither of us is afraid to voice our opinion to others about how to get us there. Sound like a combination for disaster? Yep, you got that right, folks! I realized I gave him too many choices and too many chances yet didn't have a consistent follow-up procedure for discipline in various situations—whether I was at home, shopping in the store, or at a neighborhood park.

One day, Devon did not want to clean his room before dinner when asked. In a fit of defiance, he dumped out every well-organized, labeled bin of toys into one pile—Thomas the Tank Engine trains and tracks, building blocks, books, puzzles, etc. I peeked over the bottom half of the locked Dutch door to witness a heap of expensive (and once organized) toys, literally piled as high as Devon. I waited for Phil to come home—because I wanted him to witness Devon's rage and so we could discipline him together.

I easily could have **enabled** him by putting the mess away myself, but instead, I chose to **empower** him by teaching him through his experience and his anger. Later, we calmly explained that it was unfortunate he had made these choices. We explained that everything had to be put back where it belonged, and we were available to help. By connecting his choice with the consequences, Devon began to understand that his decisions would have repercussions.

Letting a wild horse run free. Things improved, but he would still have stubborn flare-ups. And when Devon flared, I flared. Finally, I reached out to Dr. Lynne Kenney for deeper psychological direction. She shared the analogy of training a horse. Once the horse is trained, it trusts you, and you trust it, so you can give the horse a larger arena to run in. When you give the horse clear direction, you can allow it the freedom to run *within* the arena (but not to run wild *outside* it).

As a child, I learned best through analogies, and this one made sense to me. I tightened my behavior modification plan to be like the arena—my rules, my arena. Devon was given the independence he craved to make his own decisions but within my parameters. For example, when it came time to dress for church, I gave him the choice between two outfits. He thrived knowing he had a voice, and it could be heard. We both agreed that when tensions rose, it was helpful for us to take some deep breaths and talk calmly, clearly, and respectfully to each other.

 Rope of Connection

As humans, we have daily connections with people from family, to teachers, fellow students, and our community. We must learn how to respectfully interact with others, represent ourselves, and behave accordingly and age appropriate.

My parents were super stellar at teaching me and my sister table manners, appropriate introductions to others, how to properly answer the house phone and take a message, etc.

Most parents teach their children simple phrases such as saying "please" and "thank you." We can build on that beginning by also teaching our children to behave appropriately in a nice restaurant, to offer help when others need it, and act properly when meeting new people.

The phrase that pays. To reinforce these behaviors, when the boys were as young as four, I would pay them 25 cents for each of the following things they did correctly during an introduction: look the adult in the eye, give a firm handshake (or wave when they were in pre-school), and say, "Nice to meet you, Mr. or Mrs. Whomever." It became a creative game to see how many "manner moments" they would have when we met people and was also a unique way for them to learn the value of money and earn it in a fun, respectable way!

Now, at ages 9 and 12, they have nailed it! They exude confidence in themselves and are respectful to others they encounter. In addition, this game has "paid off big time," for it also helped them in situations like presenting in the classroom or being interviewed by judges for a Science Fair Project. Who knew?! I would be a very wealthy mama if I were to add up the gazillion times each week that people tell me how well-behaved, polite, and well-mannered my boys are. I couldn't beam any brighter or be any prouder. We invested a few years to develop these manners, and it is so very worth it!

Epic Organizing Adventure: Manners to Model After

Clearly discuss <u>and</u> demonstrate how <u>you</u> would like your child to <u>greet</u> others when you <u>introduce</u> them. For example, before I walk into the print center to pick up my brochures, I tell Oliver, "I am going to introduce you to meet Mrs. Anderson who handles my print work. When I introduce you, remember to offer her a firm handshake, wide smile and look her in the eye when you say, "Nice to meet you Mrs. Anderson." You will do great, sweetie!

Do 5 introductions to someone they know <u>casually</u>, then 5 introductions to <u>someone new</u>. Be sure to honor their hard work with what you agreed upon as rewards!

___1 ___2 ___3 ___4 ___5 ___6 ___7 ___8 ___9 ___10

 ## Water Bottle

It is essential for our kids to understand overall food health and nutrition and how their choices impact their bodies.

I never realized the importance of teaching about health and nutrition until my younger child, Oliver, was born. After several years of health challenges, we eventually met with naturopathic guru, Dr. Suneil Jain, who discovered that Oliver had multiple food allergies and intolerances. The clean eating program he recommended has changed our family life. Phil had had some similar issues, and his ailments have also been resolved through

Dr. Jain's direction. I state in humor but speak in truth that we are a "special needs food family." Reading food labels with our kids is not only part survival—it's educational and very entertaining!

We make a game of it by trying to guess how much sugar is in a certain product, or how the food company is trying to trick us with their marketing on nutrition. Phil and I often discuss what whole, fresh food is, and how it differs from packaged, processed food.

Epic Organizing Adventure: Reading Food Labels

We talk to the boys about different ingredients to watch out for (like sugars and salts), so they can be well-educated shoppers. Now they are knowledgeable enough to share with other kids why certain foods are better choices and make healthy food decisions when we are not with them.

Read together 10 food labels that currently are in your pantry.

___1___2___3___4___5___6___7___8___9___10

Read together 10 food labels in the grocery store.

___1___2___3___4___5___6___7___8___9___10

Time to scream from the mountain top in shear PRIDE! Woohoo! Together, you have covered miles of some mighty ground!

 You have learned to Empower and not Enable your adventurous kiddo and earned another stack of clutter-free coins to keep your organizing game strategy strong if you successfully completed the following:

- ❏ You've reviewed each of the following life skills icons and discussed with your child how it relates to organizing.
    - ✷ Compass
    - ✷ Binoculars
    - ✷ Home Tent
    - ✷ Map
    - ✷ Notebook & Pencil
    - ✷ Rope of Connection
    - ✷ Rocky Mountain
    - ✷ Water Bottle
- ❏ You strive to set an example for your children and empower rather than enable them.
- ❏ Although some days are rough and rocky, you end up feeling pretty AWESOME as a parent, knowing you're helping your kiddo develop the skills required for their life's backpack and personally prepared for the adventures that lie ahead of them.

The best is yet to come! I hope you are beginning to see the relationship with your child mold into a different form than was shaped before. Now we are ready to roll into How to R.O.C.K. at Discipline.

7

HOW TO R.O.C.K. AT DISCIPLINE

In the previous chapter, we talked about empowering our children. One of the ways we do this as parents is to have clear expectations and consistent discipline.

If I sentenced Devon to the traditional time-out, he would be resourceful and find a way to amuse himself in the corner—epic discipline fail number one. If I spanked him with a pancake spatula, like my parents did to my sister and me when we were young, Devon would literally laugh and say he didn't feel anything—epic discipline fail number two.

I implemented a tremendous amount of parent and discipline mindsets from the internationally renowned psychologist Dr. Kevin Lehman's books: *Making Children Mind Without Losing Yours*[2] and *First-Time Mom;*[3] however, I still had some outstanding issues that needed resolving with Devon.

I then proceeded to read a variety of family/parenting books, and frankly, they were all either too complicated to follow

---

[2] Leman, Dr. Kevin. *Making Children Mind Without Losing Yours*. Baker Publishing Group, 2004.

[3] Leman, Dr. Kevin. *First-Time Mom: Getting off on the Right Foot from Birth Through First Grade*. Tyndale House Publishers, 2004

or would not apply to Devon and his mature mindset. After countless hours researching and trying different discipline methods, I elected to flat out create my own ... lightbulb moment, right?

Once we decided upon and started to implement our own approach, Phil and I found it was easier to follow, and it could be applied to an endless number of situations. In our home, we now use the R.O.C.K. method of discipline:

R – Request
O – One Warning
C – Consequence
K – Kindness

From head to toe, God blessed Devon, now 12, with the most analytical of brains and the largest of feet. He is gifted-level smart, highly organized, and can hyper-focus on the tasks at hand. This means at times he is disobedient because he wants to do things in his obsessively methodical way.

This contrasts with how his younger brother is programmed and often results in disagreements. Doing things his way can have benefits. It is commonplace to find Devon completely dressed and ready for the day by 6 a.m., all on his own. But his headstrong personality tends to make him only approach things the way he desires, whether that falls within our rules or not.

Here is an example of how R.O.C.K. applied outside the home during a typical outing to Target when the boys were younger. Before we entered the store, I told them that if they were good helpers while shopping and didn't bicker or goof off, I would treat them to a delicious chocolate milk at checkout. Devon, being the eldest, wanted to push the cart. I was fine with that, but I explained the shopping cart road rules.

R = Request

Mommy: Devon, you must stay on the right side of the aisles to avoid traffic jams with the other customers. You cannot race around with the cart like a crazy person either, because you might hurt someone. Do you understand?

Devon: Yes, Mommy, he answers with the excitement of a slug.

Devon then proceeded to drive the shopping cart his way, almost bumping into a toddler playing on the next aisle over. This was when we started with *R—Request.* I asked that Devon pay better attention and remember the rules for driving the cart so he could get his treat.

Mommy: Devon, you need to watch where you are going. You could have run over and hurt that little boy. Is there something you would like to tell the boy?

Devon: Sorry, I didn't mean to hit you.

Mommy: Devon, I am *requesting* you stop goofing off and start focusing on being safe. Do you understand?

NOTE: In order to get his full attention, I often bend down to be at his eye level and put my hand on his shoulder, so he sees me, feels me, and can hear me.

Devon: Yes, Mommy.

O = One Warning

About 10 minutes later, I noticed Devon's memory apparently was wiped clean of the toddler incident because he continued to jump on the cart and ride it even faster down the next aisle. He nearly collided into the cart of someone's sweet grandma. We now moved on to *O—One Warning*.

Mommy: Devon, I *requested* earlier you drive the cart safely, but you are still goofing off. So now you've moved to O. This is your *One Warning*. If you don't start listening, then you have chosen to move to C. Your *Consequence* will be not getting chocolate milk with your brother at the cafe after checkout. Do you understand? Your *choice*, sweetie!

Devon: Yes, Mommy, he answered, this time in a more frustrated tone.

Mommy: If you continue to goof off before we reach the cashier, then you earned your *Consequence*. Do you understand?

Devon: Yes, Mommy! I got it!

Mommy: Remember, this is *your choice,* not mine, so make it a good one!

Side note: Often, younger brother Oliver will help Devon stay on track. Ollie likes to follow rules, and when treats are involved, he is even more willing to help his brother make it happen. I am completely fine with them being supportive of each other. But if they *both* goof off, then they *both* face the consequences. No exceptions!

C = **Consequence**

We approached the checkout and Devon once again behaved irresponsibly. His *C—Consequence* kicked in. He was surprisingly shocked but equally mad and crossed his arms in stubbornness. We approached the café, and only Oliver was awarded his chocolate milk treat. Devon looked the other way while blaming everyone else for his poor choices under his breath.

Devon was quite upset, as he should have been, so I told the boys no talking was allowed on the car ride home. I played relaxing music to keep the mood calm and observed Devon glaring out the window, peeved about his choices. We arrived home, and both boys helped unload the car and put away our recently purchased supplies.

K = **Kindness**

It was now time for the final step in my R.O.C.K. Method, which is *K—Kindness*. I held Devon's hand as we moved into his bedroom. I gave him a big hug and kiss saying, "I am so sorry you made those choices and, unfortunately, got the consequence. Take a few breaths to calm down, and I will check back in a few minutes to see how you are doing."

Devon continued to show anger and frustration and proceeded to slam his bedroom door. In our home, if a door is slammed shut out of anger, one dollar is owed to the family bank. Oh, geez, another consequence.

But, again, we were working on behavior, choices, and self-control. If Devon was still an angry mess, I gave him another supportive hug, another kiss, and we prayed together. I then proceeded to help him get back on his feet, and when he was ready, he helped the family set the table for dinner.

Some days are as smooth as satin, while others are as rough as ROCKS. Regardless, this is a simple and consistent discipline strategy to implement when needed, and it helps us keep our daily rhythm rolling along.

The more informed children are about *the choices* presented to them in any given situation, the better able they are to exercise age-appropriate decision-making and self-control. Eventually, the repetition inspires positive choices in their actions and/or behavior.

Through Dr. Kenney's guidance, I learned how to work with a strong-willed, bright child, like Devon. The technique involved visually imagining a horse corral. I can allow Devon to run free in the corral, as long as he exhibits appropriate behavior. In the story above, Target is that corral. When given clearly defined *choices* for behavior (that would be rewarded with chocolate milk), he is given *control* over how to use the cart and is also aware of the *consequences* if he chooses poorly.

Handling Meltdowns

Often a child has a meltdown because of the consequences of their choices, and it's common to hear parents tell the frustrated child to "use your words." This is rarely successful when they are very young. It's important for parents to remember that children are still learning how to understand the swirling emotions inside them. They don't yet have the verbal skills to explain what they can't comprehend.

It is our role as parents to help them *find* the words to *express* their emotions. We have to work with them to *identify* and *describe* what they are feeling. This patience and guidance will help them better communicate what they are feeling. Once they are able to *describe* their feelings, they are on the way to *understanding* behavior expectations and choices.

Eventually, these efforts will result in your child understanding *how* to express their emotions effectively, which leads to greater responsibility and self-control in a variety of circumstances. They'll learn to manage a series of situations successfully, such as behaving appropriately in public, promptly dressing in the morning, putting dishes away the first time they're asked, or being a respectful student during class time. These successes develop greater confidence and pride.

A tight-knit, dependable family unit plays a role in this process as well. It is so great to see when the family begins to work together in a cohesive and communicative way. The entire family thrives and rises together. The results are beautiful and beneficial for everyone—every day and for always!

Role-Play and Praise Often

What kid does not like to pretend to be the parent? Exactly! Give the kids a chance to act out how your newly decided R.O.C.K. Method or selected discipline strategy would play out once put in effect.

I recall it was bona fide hilarious when we did this with the boys! We may have even taped it on the iPad to watch back a few times as well. It might be fun to reverse the roles, making the kids the parents and vice versa.

Role-playing sheds a soft light on a topic that families often find themselves in the dark over. It provides a chance to discuss and get feedback on strategies in a fun way that encourages dialogue and understanding. More importantly, it's being done during a quiet time and not in the middle of a disciplinary moment.

Families need to take the time to discuss discipline strategies thoroughly, so everyone understands their purpose. Once that foundation is set, the strategies need to be consistently implemented. The final step is often overlooked. When new behaviors and habits start to develop, don't forget to notice and praise one another!

Epic Organizing Adventure: R.O.C.K. Method Activities

An innovative way for everyone to remember the R.O.C.K. Method is to do an activity together where each letter is represented. Review some suggestions below or create your own based on your child's age and creativity level

Color the R.O.C.K. Method Printable – Download the printable from WurthOrganizing.com, and set aside time to decorate it together. Post the decorated printable in a noticeable location, such as the kitchen fridge or playroom, as a reminder and reference.

Create your own R.O.C.K. Collection – Search around your home to find four medium-sized rocks. Then, decorate each rock with one letter! You may want to color in letters from the printable or design your own using gel or metallic Sharpie markers. You could print them on sticker paper or cut out and glue a letter on each rock using Mod Podge or white glue. Select a visible location such as the kitchen windowsill or child's shelf so they are a visual prompt that can be reflected upon.

Make Edible Rocks – For those more interested in eating than crafting, take a vote on what yummy treat you shall make together using the R.O.C.K. letters. Use cookie cutters to cut out each letter on a baking sheet or spell each letter on top of a batch of brownies using M & M's. It's all about bonding and learning the R.O.C.K. Method together.

You've learned how to R.O.C.K. at Discipline and earned another stack of clutter-free coins to keep your organizing game strategy strong if you successfully completed the following:

- ❑ You and your family have developed a consistent and mutually agreed upon discipline strategy. This may be the R.O.C.K. Method, or perhaps one you create for your family dynamic.
- ❑ You and your family have written down this strategy, step-by-step, so that everyone is aware of and understands each step. For example, when using R.O.C.K., everyone understands the sequence of expectations and consequences.
- ❑ Your family's discipline strategy has been printed and posted where it can be seen by you and the children, as well as any grandparents, babysitters, and others who may be involved in your children's lives.
- ❑ You and your family have role-played your discipline strategy. You have found solutions that work or ones that need readjusting by thoroughly discussing them together. You take great care to implement a discipline consistency over time.

- ❏ Praise is given to *all* family members when appropriate behavior and healthy choices are made. Remember that both the child *and* parent mature when implementing a discipline strategy, and self-control is expected from *both* parties.
- ❏ You have engaged in either a crafty or tasty activity together to help represent the R.O.C.K. Method. Pictures are encouraged and memories made as you spend time growing closer together.

As we progress to the next chapter, it's time to get super cheddar cheesy!

Read out loud the following to your child:

"Who has rhythm?
I sure do!
Then let's get systems grooving for both me and you!"

Be prepared for either a smile, a hug, or a serious eye roll from your child (depending on how cheesy they think you are!). It's all good!

8

DAILY SYSTEMS AND RHYTHMS

Whether we realize it or not, everyone's daily life has a preset rhythm that dictates how our precious 24 hours are spent. No matter our age or season of life, that framework is consistent for everyone, everywhere, all over the world.

Every morning, we wake up, get dressed, eat meals, and go to work or learn or serve others. As our day ends, we prepare for the following one and eventually go to sleep so that we can, hopefully, wake up and do it all again.

I have always found this common framework fascinating and, at the same time, encouraging. Consistent routines are an important part of life and can help create a healthy balance for daily living. When we intentionally devise daily routines and rhythms, it relieves us mentally from always having to plan the next step.

Routines give us a sturdy structure around which to plan the day. The more often and intentionally we lean upon our routines, the more natural it becomes, and the more confidence you can strut as you see the hours in your days seamlessly move forward.

Driven to Distraction

When I initially kicked off Wurth Organizing, I had the great pleasure of connecting with, and eventually be mentored by, Dr. Lynne Kenney. You met her earlier, remember? She emphasizes the importance of developing easy-to-follow, consistent routines for daily family life. The benefit of these routines is evident for those with traditional functional minds and those blessed with distractible attention deficit disorder (ADD) minds.

I personally have Attention Deficit/Hyperactivity Disorder (ADHD) and awake each day with a mind that works at an intense pace. Ideas fly at me at 200 miles per hour, like an Indy car on its racetrack. But the idea of routines creating a structure led to a life-changing epiphany.

Make your energy match your efficiency. While my ADHD mind and energy are in endless supply, my efficiency and output can be weak because it's just too dang exhausting to keep up with the ideas. I realized it was in my best interest to move forward on life's freeway using a Routine Chore Chart rather than wasting energy and gas driving in a reckless circle on the track. The crash-and-burn option clearly wasn't appealing!

When creating my own chore chart, I recognized that pairing daily tasks together made sense. I would complete one task, and that would trigger the start of a complementary task to be done next.

For instance, after my morning prayer time, I make the bed and put my jammies in the nightstand drawer. Like a classic peanut butter and jelly combo, certain routines work well together every time. My simple routine chart not only helped my distractible mind "focus and finish" one task at a time, but it also became a clever tool for my kiddos, which leads me right into my next point!

Routine Chore Chart

Our younger son Oliver has always been a rule follower. When I say, "Ok, Ollie, time to turn off your show," his immediate response is to reply, "Ok, Mommy." This is a refreshing change from Devon's usual protest. But, like all children, Ollie came with his own set of challenges. He is a loving, creative, and distractible spirit. He earned the nickname "one shoe wonder" because he could walk around for an hour with one shoe on and one off or one sock on and one off.

How the concept was born. Ollie's challenge was for him to *stay focused to finish a task,* any task. Since I am a self-proclaimed "recovering perfectionist," I elected to focus my time on teaching these life skills to my boys instead of spending time on a fancy-schmancy chore chart. Developing a chore chart helped *both* boys because it kept Ollie focused so he can finish his morning routine and gave his older brother Devon an opportunity to use his leadership skills and guide Ollie through the routine.

My challenge was to create something that would *engage* him, *guide* him. Dr. Kenney mentioned how mastering daily routines and responsibilities is a constant challenge for many of her clients—of all ages. With her inspiration, this new-found knowledge spurred me on to design a compact, customizable, yet visual and interactive Routine Chore Chart that works for people of all ages.

- Basically, it is a laminated 6 x 9 image with sky-write lines, where daily tasks are written using a Sharpie marker.
- Colored Post-it® flags are placed on each task line, so when my son completes a task (such as brushing his teeth or making the bed), the flag is moved from one side to the other.
- The boys selected the location of their chart, under the light switch in their bathroom. I simply adhered it to the wall using removable 3M Command™ Picture Hanging Strips. Simple and fun to implement. DONE!
- Dr. Kenney loved the product so much she purchased more than 40 of them to give to her client families! The chart tasks can be easily removed with a wet magic eraser and can be used and reused endlessly.

Routine ideas worth repeating. When Ollie was too young to read, I wrote in the task and drew a picture of the corresponding icon beside it. For example, the Get Dressed task showed a shirt, and the Brush Teeth task showed a toothbrush. I could have spent hours on Pinterest to find and create some fancy, cutesy board, but I decided it felt better to get it *done* than to get it *perfect*.

Working on new routines together via trial and error can also bring your family closer. Before heading out the door, a leave-no-family-member-behind mentality takes over, and everyone pitches in so you can get out the door on time each morning.

Stan-the-non-routine-man. Take, for example, one of our clients, Stan. He's a single dad who exemplifies the Formerly

Known as Organized personality type. Stan used to be married with a consistent work and travel routine. However, as a single dad, his schedule has become less regular since he moved to a different home, and his job schedule has changed. He no longer has a consistent routine from one week to the next.

Consequently, every day presents new and unexpected challenges. He feels like he never knows what's coming next and must move at Mach speed to try to keep up, rushing from one last-minute task with his twin girls to the next.

A typical day may involve Stan realizing around lunchtime that his twin girls have karate practice that night. Since he didn't plan ahead, he doesn't have their gear, so he leaves work early to dash home and pick up their uniform bags, which makes him late for school pickup.

Stan is normally an organized person when it comes to work, but this type of after-school planning is something his wife used to handle. He now needs to devise a *new* rhythm that works for his *new* family life.

The girls quickly change into their uniforms, and as Stan is driving the girls to practice, they realize no one packed snacks or water bottles. The twins did not think to remind him because they were not taught to be empowered by their parents.

By now, everyone is hungry and on short fuses from the stress of rushing. Stan pulls into a local gas station to grab some sugary, last-minute snacks instead of the healthy banana and granola bar they might have eaten if he had planned ahead. The unnecessary stops meant the girls arrived late to practice, rushed and barely fed.

Stan walks back to his car, takes a deep breath, and then realizes he has no plans for dinner after practice. He rushes to the nearest grocery store to pick up last-minute dinner items only to find some of his recent grocery purchases were already stocked in his pantry.

Today's "ticket cost" for being Formerly Known as Organized is now more than $25. Stan sits down at the dinner table too exhausted for family chitchat. He knows he can't chug along at this pace for much longer, and he also knows he isn't setting any fine examples for his kiddos. Stan and his family would undoubtedly benefit from a Routine Chore Chart.

Imagine if the girls shared responsibility for ensuring their uniform gear was in Dad's car before they left for school, and they packed snacks and filled their water bottles the night before? Not only would the twins feel empowered helping Dad plan their days, but what great habits he would be teaching to his daughters. It's all possible with the creation of a Routine Chore Chart.

Setting Routines

There are many ways that routines can be used to keep our daily rhythms in step. I love using old-fashioned, turn-dial kitchen timers. If the kids are starting to goof off in the morning, and I see the time ticking away, I announce: "Okay, Mommy is setting the timer. You have 10 minutes to do your morning routine chore and report to the hallway! If the timer goes off and you are not ready, there will be a consequence."

Suddenly, the kids shift from goof-off time to get yourself in gear like a gladiator ready for battle, or you will lose and be eaten when the tigers are set loose in the Roman Coliseum. With little tricks like this, it's possible to make organizing fun and not militant.

Make systems simple and requests reasonable.

One thing to remember: we all live under the same family tent and need to support one another. For instance, come morning time, if one child gets their lunch packed and in their backpack early, they are expected to assist their sibling or other family members pack up for the day.

Every morning is an all-hands-on-deck situation where everyone needs to do their part to be sure the boys get to school on time, and we can begin our workday on time. The goal is to have everyone leave at an expected time to head out for the day!

Epic Organizing Adventure: Routine Chart Creation

Now that you're ready to start your own routines, take a moment to print out my snazzy **Routine Chore Chart.** You can find it on my website **WurthOrganizing.com.** You can enlarge or minimize the size and then laminate it for endless use.

1. Decide if you desire a Morning or Evening Routine Chart. Maybe you'd like to create both.
2. Have your child select the color of the Sharpie permanent marker you will use to write out each task.

3. Clearly write a single task per line in large print. For younger children who can't read or older folks who require glasses, draw a simple outline image to identify the required task. For example, in addition to writing "make bed," draw a bed, or for "get dressed," draw a shirt.
4. Don't worry about being perfect. What's most important is that the tasks that are expected to be done are on the list, and there is an awareness that everyone keeps each other accountable.
5. The big finish involves finding a place to post the chart. I like to put it in a visible location where it can be easily referenced by both the big and little people in the house.

Behavior Modification Chart

If there was a chart that made the biggest impact (ironically) on MY behavior toward my kiddos, it was this one! The **Behavior Modification Chart** can also be found on my website.

When Devon was in kindergarten, his teacher used this Behavior Modification Chart for each student, every day. The concept was literally kindergarten basic yet brilliant at the same time.

A huge vertical rainbow poster was placed in front of the classroom. Every child's name was written on a clothespin, which was clipped on the green section at the start of each school day. If a student exhibited *positive* behaviors in the classroom or on the playground, the teacher *moved their clip up* to the pink section, then blue, and eventually purple. However, if they exhibited *negative* behaviors, their clip *moved down* to the yellow section, then orange and eventually red.

Devon loved this program (and so did I), so we immediately began enforcing it at home by coloring in the center column of my nifty Routine Chore Chart in the same respective color order. I used binder clips instead of clothespins because I AM an organizer, and it just made sense!

Since Devon and I have very similar personalities, emotions can easily flare up or down between us. To hold myself accountable, we paired ourselves together on one chart and Phil and Ollie on another. Both charts were posted by the homework table in the kitchen, where most of the action goes down.

If I exhibited negative behavior in the car or at home by snapping impolitely at the kids, they had the authority to "make Mommy clip down." If I did something special with them like play a round of Uno or have a popcorn picnic in the backyard, they could clip me up.

Hands down, this was one of the most effective behavior solutions for our entire family! It encouraged us to monitor our behavior and self-control.

Seriously, give it a go in your household and see what happens. The results are likely to surprise you as much as they did me. It's a great way to stay consistent and accountable and sane.

You have incorporated Daily Systems and Rhythms and earned another stack of clutter-free coins to keep your organizing game strategy strong by successfully completing the following:

- ❑ Printed off, personalized, and posted a Routine Chore Chart (or created one of your own) to keep your children and yourself on track each day.
- ❑ Worked as a family team with "all-hands-on-deck" at least 10 times to accomplish daily tasks and had some fun not taking yourselves too seriously as you learned together.
- ❑ Discussed at least 5 new systems that are easy to follow and then determined which requests would be reasonable to enforce.
- ❑ Avoided being driven to distraction by staying focused on what is most important, especially during the bookends of each day.
- ❑ If needed, your family has implemented a Behavior Modification Chart in your home and found learning from one another has been most helpful.

Serious strides are being made at home! The best is yet to come as you both slide straight into one of the most anticipated chapters of the book—organizing your child's bedroom. It can and will happen!

9

KIDS' ROOMS: NATURAL DISASTER OR COMFORTING SHELTER

A well-organized kid's room must include structural and systematic organizing elements to increase a child's confidence, sustain predictable order, and in turn, reduce parental insanity.

When a child's personal space lacks a functional foundation, their room is likely to reflect the environment of a recent natural disaster. Like a volcanic explosion, the hot lava of laundry, LEGOS, and leggings will eject wildly into midair, landing where they may while destroying all manner of healthy life in their destructive path.

To be honest, I've found kids generally want to feel confident about themselves and want to have pride in their surroundings. That's the perfect environment and combination for parents who want to introduce organizing skills.

Another benefit of a well-organized room is that it can decrease a child's daily frustration and anxiety. Cluttered and chaotic spaces can negatively impact their mindset. Additionally, the unpredictability of the outside world can feel like a terrifying tornado around them, from school to sports to social media pressures. The fast-swirling tornado of daily life feels like it can easily suck them up and their belongings.

Instead, work with your child to create a comforting, well-organized personal space (safe shelter) where they can escape, refresh, and recharge. This is smart parenting. The tornado will always move at warp speed and in unpredictable directions; therefore, it's important to have a consistent, calm shelter.

Offering the experience of a consistent, yet comfortable space in their family home to retreat to will be greatly beneficial as they grow older. They'll know how to make a space their own and avoid unhealthy ways of seeking comfort, such as food, online media, excessive gaming, vaping, online shopping, or opioids (just to name a few). Studies have even shown that a child's developing brain can be permanently altered as a result of disorder in their room and disorganized home lifestyles.

Creating Order

My son Oliver (now 9) is my Creative Collector. He loves to collect things and uses a wide variety of mechanical pencils and colored markers to organize his collections. His most recent focus has been metallic gel pens! Because he loves and appreciates many types of items, Oliver and I spend time together each month reassessing his overjoyed collection of schoolwork and knickknacks.

My son Devon (now 12) is my sharp-minded, Methodical Mind. He likes having his personal set of tools and a complete collection of battery supplies easily accessible in his desk drawer. However, he only stores items and game sets that he truly needs for a reason and a purpose. There is an inner minimalist brewing inside him for sure.

As you can see from Oliver and Devon, kids have their own personalities they bring to organizing, and it's important that their organizing strategy suits *their* personality and not yours. That's a unique challenge for parents because you may have to adjust *your* approach for *each* child. But hopefully, you know your child better than anyone else, so I believe you're perfectly suited to the challenge, and I'll help you every step of the way.

Here are the basics and benefits all kids crave in their rooms:

- **Order.** If kids can miraculously maintain order with systems at school (such as putting their backpack in their cubby and their pencil case in their desk), then this "miracle" can occur at home. Who knew? Their behavior in school proves how fully capable they are (both emotionally and physically). They should be able to transfer those skills and perform the same activities at home.
- **Structure.** Consistency in structured actions leads to mastery of habits.
- **Personality.** Personal space that reflects their individual personality style and hobby interests.
- **Space.** Physical space where they enjoy playing and exploring, either by themselves or with loved ones.
- **Organization.** Well-labeled drawers, shelves, or closet sections to avoid habitual havoc.
- **Treasures.** Kids love being surrounded by their treasures and accomplishments.

It is finally time for you and your kiddo to transform your first space together, and I know you are ready! You already learned how to Master the 4 A's of Organizing in chapter 4, and now those steps can be fully put into action. You're going to see how effective each phase is and why it is effective when used in the proper order.

ASSESS PHASE

Before starting any project, you need to take time to **assess both the space and its function.**

In my first book, I used a baseball analogy to explain this important overall organizing game plan of all 4 Organizing Phases. I talked about how it's important to tag all bases to score a home run in any home space. The most common mistake I see in disorganized clients is that they skip the crucial first step (a.k.a. first base). Instead, everyone wants to sprint straight to step three (a.k.a., third base) where items are assigned a new system and placed in organizing containers and baskets, therefore skipping the Attack Phase (a.k.a. second base)

Don't fall into this trap. Take the extra time and follow the steps in the proper order. Stay strong and know that going step-by-step will result in a functional solution that will work, not just for today or next week, but for a total "home run" solution (not an epic fail strikeout).

NOTE: Use this important time during the Assess Phase to pause and reflect. Look at the space with your child and note what works and what doesn't. You child will greatly appreciate the time and interest you're taking in their space, and in turn, this will likely strengthen your relationship. As

I have said before, I believe organizing has mysterious and magical powers. You'll see these benefits as you progress through the book ... you'll see.

Assessment Strategy

Picture the potential. Part of understanding how you and your child want to use the space and what steps will be needed to get there involves obtaining an objective view of the space. The best way to get this perspective is by taking photos of the space in all its glory from multiple angles so you have a 360-degree view. Remember dressers, armoires, closets, and desk/craft areas, if applicable. Upload pictures of the space into a well-labeled album via a free app, such as Dropbox™. Photos of your space are helpful and can be motivating for future reference. They're also great for bragging rights, so you can show before and after pictures once you have ignited the organizers in you and your child.

Sketch it out. Do a quick, rough sketch of the space, furniture and room dimensions, with a traditional measuring tape. Be conservative in your findings by rounding down your numbers to the nearest 1/8 of an inch. Note obstructions for areas you need to work around, such as an electrical panel on the wall, windows, and doors.

Progress over paralysis. Maybe the space looks like an episode on The Weather Channel, featuring natural disasters. Are you frozen in fear? This will be the last time this space will require an environmental clean-up crew to revitalize it from its current condition. You will move forward and continue to push on through these pages, my friend. Push on!

How is your child currently using this space? What works and what doesn't? There is a strong emotional and psychological connection between children, their belongings, and their private rooms. Are they sporty? An avid reader? Do they enjoy sleepovers or game time with friends?

What are the top 5 knots that need untangling in this space? Figure out what isn't working. Shelves too high to reach or drawers too stuffed with outgrown clothes for you both to put away clean laundry?

#1 Knot _____

#2 Knot _____

#3 Knot _____

#4 Knot _____

#5 Knot _____

What activities would your child like to do in this space? Does your child like to build, play, and create endless craft projects? Discuss and decide what vibe they want the room to have and what look will meet their needs.

Check the condition of the space in the following areas to determine if any repairs or structural/design changes need to be made:

- ❏ **Doors.** Are any broken, need repair or replacement? When we moved into our current single-level home, Devon needed significant floor space so he could build his train tracks. I noticed, month after month, that he kept the bifold doors to his closet open. This decreased floor space and prevented him from connecting all his train tracks together, which frustrated him. We discussed with him the idea of just popping the doors off the track. He liked the idea, so Phil took the doors off and stored them in the garage. Removing them not only made the room feel significantly larger, but it also gave Devon an additional 8 inches of space on each side of the closet where the doors used to be. He gained a total of 16 inches of underutilized space. As part of the deal, Devon was accountable for keeping the closet space tidy. Fast forward to today, the doors have never been reinstalled. Instead, we've passed them along to our neighbor.

❑ **Alternative Options.** If you want to gain floor space but feel your child needs the closet to be enclosed, add a window panel, beaded curtain, or trendy barn door to cover the closet opening.

❑ **Shelving.** There are endless floating shelf options on the market to house keepsakes; however, before installing, I suggest you discuss with your child their commitment to dusting the shelves and whether the items and/or the shelf will be hit if being placed in a high-energy kiddo's space. An alternative to floating shelves is a 3-Tier Mega Expand-A-Shelf. Traditionally marketed for housing condiments in a kitchen pantry, I love to also use it for storing my boys' figurines and toy cars. This shelf expands to a generous width and sits nicely on the interior shelf in their closet.

❑ **Lighting.** Is there enough light? Can a light kit be added to an existing fan or swapped out for an adjustable track light system?

❑ **Designer Eye.** For a $100 consultation fee, The Container Store® offers the Contained Home Program® where a highly qualified closet designer and/or professional organizer offers an in-home consultation, discussing your specific space needs, style, and budget. They oversee your entire project from in-home consultation to installation day. The designers will help you every step of the way—taking interior pictures, sketching future solutions, providing a 3D computer-aided design of a future closet, or designing a closet solution using completion products offered by The Container Store. From the modular Elfa hanging system to the European style Avera line or their upscale Laren Closet line.

My team of gurus and I are proud to be the Official Brand Partner of The Container Store, where we oversee all three Valley locations in Arizona!

ATTACK PHASE

The Attack Phase can be the toughest time during the organization process. It's where you *attack and dissect* what you are keeping, mending, consigning, donating, or gifting. Depending on the intensity of the volume, this phase may require multiple rounds due to the multiple layers collected over so many weeks or years.

Mentally, this is the toughest time for folks. You are starting to *move into motion,* but if you follow my simple task list below, you will see huge progress in a very short amount of time. I promise it will feel like a dropping-5-pounds-fast type of dreamy!

Nonnegotiable Steps and Why They Matter

Be sure to include your child in this clean-up process. It is important that children are equally affected by the raw state of affairs in their space. No fingers are to be pointed or blame to be shared any further. That was then, and this is now. We're moving forward! Exercise appropriate emotional self-control and silently work together. This is a period of "repair." Avoid making a deeper "tear" in your existing relationship. Focus on what to do with the items in the room. Don't get distracted by doing any detailed cleaning of furniture or belongings … we will get to that later!

Set the appropriate expectations for the project. Remember, their space didn't become this tangled tornado in one hour, so don't expect it to be resolved in one hour. It *will* get completed by following my guide. And I guarantee you *both* will be forever changed in how you think about the space and all its belongings once complete. There is tremendous *value in the experience* and your perspective adjusting to it *and* through it. Embrace it all!

***Pause* to celebrate since there is a *cause* to celebrate.** Did you only pause to celebrate your child's math skills during their elementary years but not during their preschool years? Of course not, because *each* lesson learned was a "cause to celebrate."

The same celebratory attitude applies when ANY small task is completed, and they are ALL worth celebrating together. You will see the phrase "Pause for Celebration" on the list below. Rotate who decides the next celebration activity. It could be dancing to a favorite song, sharing a yummy treat, or taking a silly selfie video! The small celebrations can keep the inner fire burning for you both.

Happy notes. We love Pharrell Williams' song, "Happy." I know my boys would be motivated by watching the music video and dancing around placing the newly empty box over our head in a silly celebration. Make this moment and future moments memorable for you and your kiddo.

Every minute matters. Set a timer and make it as enjoyable as possible. Tell jokes and avoid being pouty and perfectionistic. The best is truly yet to come! Sometimes, with kids especially, *only* the minutes matter, so just keep chipping away each day. Ten minutes here and 20 minutes there will get you closer to the finish line … there truly is one, I promise you that!

Steps to Take

Whether or not your child's belongings are spread like hot lava over their bedroom and closet floor, you will quickly see "dreamy results" by taking the following steps:

1. **Gather the following supplies in your working area:**
   - ❑ (1) Organizing Tool Kit
   - ❑ (3) Solid Plastic Tubs
   - ❑ (6) Banker Boxes
   - ❑ (4) Handled Shopping Bags
   - ❑ (2) Stellar Smiles
   - ❑ *Pause for Celebration!*

2. **Label the plastic tubs "items to be sorted."**
   - ❑ Scoop (or shovel) everything from the floor quickly into your plastic totes.
   - ❑ *Pause for Celebration!*

3. **Clean the floor.**
   - ❏ Do a quick sweep or vacuum of the entire floor space to avoid an unwelcome attack from the gnarly dust bunny brigade that has resided for too long on your child's bedroom and closet floor.
   - ❏ *Pause for Celebration!*

4. **Assemble 6 banker boxes.**
   - ❏ Scan the items in the 3 plastic "to be sorted" tubs and identify at least 6 main themes—such as, Clothing, Books, Belongs Elsewhere, Furry Friends, Toys, Tech, Trinkets & Treasures, School/Artwork, or Memory Keeping (a topic we will cover in detail in a separate chapter called Conquer Memory Mayhem).
   - ❏ Reach for a Post-it Note, binder clip, and marker from your Organizer Tool Kit. Jot down the theme on the Post-it Note and temporarily attach it to the front of the box using a binder clip (therefore not ruining the box since the themes for each one will likely change at some point.)
   - ❏ *Pause for Celebration!*

5. **Grab 4 sturdy shopping bags or line a banker box with a garbage bag and mark each accordingly:**
   - ❏ Donations: for your local thrift store, friends, or family
   - ❏ Consignment or private sale posting
   - ❏ Memory Bin or Maybe Pile of Misfits
   - ❏ Grab a trash can, and you're ready to roll!
   - ❏ *Pause for Celebration!*

6. **Go through the first "to be sorted" tub, sorting items into their respective labeled bag or box.**
    - ❏ Sort the second plastic tub in the same manner until emptied.
    - ❏ Sort the last remaining tub until all tubs are sorted accordingly.
    - ❏ *Pause for Celebration!*

Mystery pieces mania. You are likely to come across "Mystery Pieces" from games, outfits, or random broken hardware. Place these items in a labeled shoebox or Ziploc bag until the sorting and future organizing phase is 100 percent complete. At that point, they can be returned to their original set, repaired, or tossed (if no longer needed).

Everything has value. As you sort and go through items, instill the concept in your child that all things have value to someone, somewhere, in some way. However, that does *not* mean they *all* need to have value to *your child*. Encourage them to think about letting someone else enjoy things no longer needed or used. It's good to pass things on that are no longer being used or appreciated.

Especially for kids and parents, it's good to remember that if kids no longer wear or readily play with something, then it is clutter. No, *still* don't try to justify it. It *IS* clutter. If you and/or your child have trouble letting go of unused items, then head back to the Four A's chapter and reread the Attack Phase section. Read it again and again, until you both are crystal clear on this concept.

Focus and Finish

We are now ready to *focus on and finish* specific categories found in a child's room. I'll start with clothing, then progress in the next chapter to handling toys, trinkets, and treasures, and finish with stuffed animals. If you or your child prefers a different order, then do so!

Sorting Clothes Frameworks

In my other book, I organized clothes into sorting frameworks *(The Clutter-Free Cruise Method* and *The Magical Measurement Method)* to help expedite the decision-making process. In order to appeal to your kiddo, I have renamed these frameworks to *The Galactic Explosion Method* (G.E.M.) or *The Mathematical Magician Method (M.M.M.).*

I suggest you or your child read aloud each method below to decide which one they prefer. Be creative and customize the dialogue for their age-appropriate interests:

The Galactic Explosion Method

Imagine that the Captain of your family's Galactic Starship announces on the loudspeaker that the ship has been infected with a cosmic cluttering chemical, and the starship will explode into outer space within the next 30 minutes. Your parent has that time to help you select your top favorite *Galactic Gear* that you want to pack with you as you travel safely to the next nearby planet. May the organizing force be with you!

The Mathematical Magician Method

You are a famous traveling magician with shows at schools, so you need a well-organized wardrobe to house all your favorite costumes and props.

Your crafty hands shall measure the bar of your *Magician's Wardrobe* using your magical measuring tape to transform:

* Each 1 inch of linear bar space = 1 hanging item. (For example, 30 inches of tops + 30 inches of bottoms = 60 inches of space to store 60 items.)
* 1 inch of vertical shelf or drawer space is equivalent to 1 folded item.

Ready to bust out your abracadabra calculator to see what organizing magic you can make in your closet space to show the kids at your next Magic Show?

EPIC ORGANIZING ADVENTURE: Choosing Your Child's Essential Pieces

After you and your child have chosen whether they are going to use the G.E.M. or M.M.M. method, it's time to get started.

You will begin sorting their *most* favorite clothing theme (such as T-shirts) to their *least* favorite theme (such as formal wear). I suggest looking at all the pieces of a single theme at once.

1. **Identify a clothing style for their lifestyle.** Sporty, comfy, or trendy all the way? Talk with your child about the style of clothing they like to wear, and the styles they would rather no longer keep.

2. **Lay each theme pile neatly on their bed so you can add or delete pieces quickly if necessary.** If an item is in the laundry, jot its name down on a single piece of bright colored paper from your Organizer Tool Kit as a reminder for it to be added to their organizing adventure.

   I think a child needs about 50 percent less inventory than an adult. They mostly will have clothes for school, play, and special occasions. Remember, they don't go to work or attend board meetings so set their inventory goal for either 38 pieces of *Galactic Gear* (versus 75 for adults) or what fits comfortably on the wardrobe bar once measured.

3. **Set a timer for 30 minutes and start the adventure.** Help your child identify the pieces that most reflect their core personality, fashion sense, and current lifestyle. Undergarments, support wear, swimwear, layering pieces, and heavy outerwear *do not apply* in the count for either method. Accessories are also excluded, including purses, crossbody bags, drawstring sports bags, boots, shoes, and sports gear.

Maybe Pile of Misfits

How should you handle the balance of their infamous Maybe Pile of Misfits? The timer has now gone off, and hopefully, their *Galactic Gear* or *Magician Wardrobe* pieces were selected. Need more time? Reset the timer for another 15 or 30 minutes to make your final choices. Snap! Double snap!

Now, let's put those banker's boxes to use and add more if required.

Your child's outstanding Maybe Pile of Misfits is likely to fall into one of the following six categories:

1. **I love this item but have outgrown it.** Clothing that is too small can be passed down to another family member or friend or saved in a memory bin. It is bittersweet when kiddos outgrow their favorite clothes, but it is a part of growing up they need to accept, so decide what to do and move to the next item.
2. **I love this item but need to grow into it.** These items need to be stored in a future wardrobe section of the closet. I usually place these with off-season clothes.
3. **Items worth your time and money to mend.** Put the item aside in a mending pile that is in a place where they don't see it. If your child continues to ask about when you are fixing an item, then you know it's important to them. If they don't ask, then your answer was given to you plain and simple.
4. **Future consignment.** Only create this pile if you will take items to a consignment store or sell them online. If neither option interests you, then simply skip this theme pile. Again, no pressure! Clothing must be stain-free and in good condition to go to the consignment shop. That means the clothes are clean and wrinkle-free with no missing buttons or broken zippers.
5. **Donatable goods for another's child's life.** This is a great opportunity to inspire your child's giving heart. Will you wear this zip-up jacket, or do you want to pass it along to another child to keep them warm this winter? Will you wear these cleats for soccer, or do you

want to pass them along to another player who needs them? By passing their personal items along to another child, you are giving your children the opportunity to make choices that will build their character, where they can see their choices uplift others. Giving choices = a giving heart.

6. **Memory pieces.** If there is a special outfit (maybe what they wore for their first family portrait?), then it can go into their memory bin. Consider taking a picture of them with the item and putting the photo in the bin instead or just keep the photo stored on your phone. No matter what you decide, do it with your child.

NOTE: Don't tally your child's missing needs until you have successfully completed the entire Attack Phase and are ready to move to the Assign Phase. Otherwise, duplicate purchasing may occur, and your organizing efforts will be wasted. Be patient. The final step of the Assign Phase involves taking note of your child's potential shopping list needs.

For those who desire more detail:

One summer, my son Ollie, then 7 years old, asked if I would help him coordinate his church outfits for the next 2 months. My heart melted as a mom but even more so as an organizer. He doesn't like feeling rushed to select his outfits on any given morning, so he wanted to plan out his outfits and not worry. I smiled all through the next hour as we enjoyed coordinating different shirts with shorts, pants, and tie ensembles on hangers.

We talked about how white, khaki, gray, and black are neutrals so they can go with anything. We collected his outfit options by hanging the shirts on a white tubular hanger and the bottoms on a clip-style hanger. I suggested we put a 25-cent metal chrome book ring (aka, loose-leaf ring) around the neck of both hangers to keep the hangers together when hung in the closet. Voila, a new system was born.

We were quite proud of our organizing teamwork that day. It was a happy blend of moments—fun mommy, happy organizer, and quality time with my son. True story! Two years later, he still uses this chrome ring-clip system, and it works so well.

ASSIGN PHASE

This phase is important for now we shall select an organizing system. You and your child will use this system to maintain and organize the inventory in their closet, shelves, and/or dresser drawers.

Go to **WurthOrganizing.com** where you will find the **Kids Clutter-Free Closet Checklist** and the **Clothing Tag Theme Printable** to print out. Now you both will begin to see *why* the Assess and Attack phases were so crucial. It allows you to slide right into this phase and start assigning places like a true pro.

Use hanging clothes dividers for inventory control. These types of plastic hanging tags are commonly used in stores to divide clothing themes into sizes or at home to organize baby clothes by month. However, I love using them for multiple purposes. For older kids, I use them to separate their clothing themes such as shirts, pants, dresses, etc. I prefer divider styles that are vertically long, since it's easier for little eager eyes to see them hanging when looked at from far below, as opposed to the rounder product that easily spins. I continue using them through elementary school age and now into adulthood.

Print, label, and cut out each tag. Once each theme is identified and working in its place for a solid week, then start laminating each one and carefully cut it out. If your child desires to add more specific themes as time progresses, then, by all means, support their organizing efforts, and use the blank hanging tag on the printable and label maker to customize.

Return items back in color order. Kiddos love color *and* crave order so give them what they want and need! Who doesn't love seeing a cheerful rainbow in their closet each day? One day, my Ollie decided to use my extra foam Xangar® clothing dividers (spacers) to separate out each colored T-shirt theme in his closet. All the red T-shirts were placed together and separated with a spacer, then all the orange and so forth. Devon followed suit because he thought it "looked cool." That was two years ago, and it's still easily maintained by both boys like it was yesterday.

File clothes back in a fashionable theme order. Similar to properly filing papers in school folders or binders, your kiddos' clothes need to be placed in proper clothing theme categories. They wouldn't haphazardly shove their jacket into someone else's locker at school, so why would they file their t-shirts back where their winter coats go? You already have the labeled clothes dividers in place, so that's where the clothes should go. If your kiddos want to have sections divided further, then label more dividers and insert accordingly!

On-the-Hanger Themes

- **Tops:** tees, tanks, blouses, button-down shirts, polo shirts, vests
- **Bottoms:** dress pants, casual pants, and jeans
- **Long hang:** tunics, short dresses, long dresses
- **Dresses:** if your child's closet doesn't offer a long hang section, then convert their long hang item to a short hang by folding the long hang over a pant hanger, therefore cutting the length of that piece in half.
- **Jackets:** dressy blazers, casual blazers, and jackets
- **Outerwear:** vests, outer jackets, and coats
- **Special Occasion Items:** gowns, suits
- **Knits:** vests, button-up cardigans, sweaters, and sweatshirts
- **Athletic Gear:** tops, bottoms, supportive garments, and gear-related accessories
- **Uniforms and Cheer Gear:** club promo clothing and sports-related gear
- **Accessories:** Ties, belts, scarves

Hanger Intervention

When in the assigning phase for a closet, it's important to discuss hangers. For Wurth Organizing, organizing with all the same color and style hangers in a closet is a flat-out nonnegotiable. Don't try to convince yourself or me otherwise! The visual cohesion is so impactful. Just trust me 1,000 percent, and you will see why I insist on this for closets. It's like wearing a dance routine outfit in cleats … it looks odd because it is odd. Your kiddo's closet will visually transform from super sad to seriously savage in under an hour.

Hanger styles. Before committing to an entire closet of hangers, check out different styles and types of hangers to figure out what you both like. Make your choice consistent and move other style or color hangers to a different space. Hanger styles should be simple for your kiddo to use, so they can hang and remove clothing easily on a daily basis. If certain styles are too frustrating on your fingers due to physical limitations, then it's best to bring a few clothing items into the store so you can select the correct style of hanger that fits their personal needs.

Adult hangers vs. child sized. Avoid buying child hangers, and buy adult size instead. Why, you ask? A child's clothing grows out of their hangers within a year. The adult size also does not damage or stretch the clothing as you might think. If you are at a crossroads for purchasing new hangers and/or adding onto existing inventory, I would go for adult size, hands down. Depending on your budget, save the child ones for a clothing theme used less often or pass along your donatable gift for an expectant mother.

Take the time to teach them. As kids enter elementary school, I suggest spending some time with them to show how to hang up a shirt properly. That means pulling the hanger through from the bottom of the shirt up to the neck, rather than forcing a hanger through the neck, which stretches out the neckline of all their nice clothing. Then show them how to clip up shorts or skirts on hangers as well.

Accept their choice of color. If your kiddo requests a crazy neon-bright hanger color then, by all means, let *them* select the color of their choosing. You can limit their choice to hangers in your existing inventory, buy a new series for their room, or even add it to their upcoming birthday or holiday gift wish list. Making these types of choices are an important part of creating their new organizational system. The more *involved* they are in planning, the more *invested input and energy* = the more likely they will remain *committed* to keeping their space organized. Human nature 101, folks!

Bare-Bones Budget: Swap out as many hangers as possible of one color or style from other closet locations to keep hanger consistency within each closet.

Moderate Budget: Plastic tubular hangers run about 10 cents each and come in a variety of fun vibrant colors, with or without accessory clips. They can give a savvy pop of style to any closet! We elected to use crystal clear hangers with metal chrome clips for clipping up dressy shorts and skirts so they could be used in EVERYONE's closets. Being a house of boys, we found there was less opportunity for clip breakage when using metal rather plastic clips over time.

Fancy-Pants Budget: Slimline velvet hangers from Joy Mangano run about $1 dollar per hanger. However, they can be a bit tricky for kiddos to take clothes on and off, so I suggest using them only for middle school ages and older. Before choosing these hangers, I would have your child try them out, either in the store or by borrowing some of yours for a test run.

BUYER BEWARE: Be wary of buying ANY type of hangers in discount stores. It's likely the die lot was inconsistent in color compared to their regular inventory. If you must, at least purchase extras so you have enough of one odd color die lot before it is sold out. Otherwise, play it safe and buy from a consistent retail supplier, like Target or The Container Store.

On the Shelf or in a Drawer

Shelf or drawer space should house clothing your child does not have the square footage to hang in a closet or items they just *prefer* to store folded such as sweatshirts or jeans.

Fold and file each theme just like you both did for the items on hangers. Place back your top nonnegotiable items first in the color order of your choosing. Because this theme of items was not included in the Attack Phase of selecting your keeper pieces for your *Galactic Explosion Method or Mathematical Measurement Method*, now is the time to truly review the remaining inventory of their personal items, such as undies, socks, and pajama sets.

Make friends with folding clothes. Folding is totally-so-not-a-big-deal! Practice a few ways to fold that work for your child and fit their shelf location or dresser drawers best. This is a basic organizational skill they will need to use for the rest of their life, so best to teach them early.

On the shelf. Always keep the finished edge facing forward because it looks cleaner to the eye and makes it easier to tell between one item and another when stacked. Place a The Home Edit® clear shelf divider between stacks to avoid each tower toppling over on one another. For smaller framed kids, fold the item once vertically, then in half. For larger frames, tri-fold the item to get a finished edge. Include your child in the label making and placement process. Use blue tape and Sharpie for temporary placement on the shelf's edge, and swap them out for official labels once all clothing themes and their locations are finalized.

In a drawer. I suggest placing the finished edge facing up; I call it *bookend-style*, much like the spine of a book facing you. Again, I highly suggest folding 'n' filing back in color order. Bottom-line, pick a folding style that fits the space and their preference. Place a clear Sterilite® shoebox to one side to create two sections. For larger drawers, place in the middle, thereby creating three sections. Use blue tape and Sharpie for temporary placement and then print off official labels once all clothing themes and their locations are finalized.

Pajamas-set burritos. I noticed some years ago that my boys liked "chucking" their sets into their drawer, so I suggested we roll each set together and secure with an office rubber band (upgrade to a colored elastic hair tie if you prefer). It was seriously the BEST thing I ever did to keep their sets together. If your child is the mix 'n' match type, they can still create their own sets and donate any extras. These make packing for a trip uber easy for everyone.

Swap all temporary labels for final ones. Once you feel the location of all inventory is working for your child's needs, start creating labels with your label maker and swapping out the temporary labels with the final ones. Involve your kids as much as possible in this final labeling process. Let them be creative when deciding whether they want all caps, all lowercase, or decorative frame styles. This is where the bonding in the relationship occurs, and great pride is taken in what you both have achieved together! Take a selfie to cherish this moment ... you will be glad you did. I hope you share it with me via social media so I can celebrate right along with you!

ACCOUNTABLE PHASE

An organized space can easily return to mayhem in literally one day. Set realistic expectations as you both become accustomed to the new systems, locations of all the clothing, and eventually, the toy themes in the entire space. If discipline continues to be a challenge, refer to the R.O.C.K. Method chapter again to guide you and your child toward healthier emotional self-control in the choices made.

Here are some simple ways to keep the space orderly over time:

Put dirty laundry in the hamper and clean clothes away. This is another simple task for your child to execute daily, but unfortunately, too many parents fail to oversee this successfully. Clean clothing can quickly become ruined once it falls and gets trampled on a messy floor. The sooner you teach your sweet kiddo how to help you put away clean laundry, the sooner they will stop putting clean clothes in the hamper out of being lazy.

Action Step: Make sure you have an ample-sized dirty clothes hamper to house only their dirty clothes. There will be a future labeled clean clothes basket that will do double-duty, housing both their clean clothes and acting as a catchall for other personal items that need to be delivered to the bedroom or bathroom. We will discuss this in more detail in the Laundry chapter.

This chapter felt like taking down an out-of-control tornado not only for me to write it, but also for you and your kiddo to conquer it. Serious celebrations are in order for everyone!!!

You've converted their room into a Comforting (and organized) Shelter and earned another stack of clutter-free coins to keep your organizing game strategy strong if you successfully completed the following:

Assess Phase

- ❑ Understand all the core needs a child craves in their space, especially your child.
- ❑ Assessed the room, the closet space, and its function.
- ❑ Door, shelving, and lighting have been reviewed and solutions discussed.

Attack Phase

- ❑ You have included your child in the cleanup process and set appropriate expectations for progress along the way.
- ❑ The floor has been cleared and cleaned. All loose items have been placed into "to be sorted" labeled bins.

- ❑ You both have attacked and dissected the following themes into their respective labeled banker boxes:

  ___ Clothing

  ___ Books

  ___ Belongs Elsewhere

  ___ Furry Friends

  ___ Toys

  ___ Tech

  ___ Trinkets & Treasures

  ___ School/Artwork

  ___ Memory Keeping

- ❑ You have "paused to celebrate" many times over whenever each box is sorted and emptied … hooray!
- ❑ A clothing sorting method was identified to review, and future hanging and folding storage locations were created.
- ❑ The Maybe Pile of Misfits has been reviewed, and a discussion was had about circling back to it at another point in time until the pile can be eliminated completely.

Assign Phase

- ❏ All hangers have been converted to the same color/style, or you are in the process of transforming it to reflect one cohesive look.
- ❏ Printed and/or purchased and labeled hanging clothes dividers by theme, separating into current season, offseason, future sizes, consign, donate, or other themes of your choice.
- ❏ Swapped temporary labels for final ones once you and your child feel comfortable and confident all systems have been identified, and items are in their proper place in the space!

Accountable Phase

- ❏ Your child has consistently put their dirty laundry in the hamper for at least one week.
- ❏ Your child has consistently put their clean laundry away in their room for at least one week.

Whooop … there it is! The rest is really downhill, easy-peezy-lemon-squeezy from here as we hop over to Toys, Trinkets and Treasures.

10

TOYS, TRINKETS, AND TREASURES

This phase can be difficult because it is multi-layered and involves all three foundational pillars. You can help your child through this process by helping them translate the emotions felt in their *heart* about certain toy sets. They can then communicate their feelings and make decisions using their *mind*, which allows their *hands* to do the work. Since this can be a tough process, I suggest starting with items they are *least* attached to and progressing to the ones that are *more* important to them. I saved **Stuffed Animal Intervention** for the last part of this chapter, for it commonly is the most emotionally challenging for either a parent or a child, however you both decide and define the order of your own organizing adventure!

Every decision is an important one because it IS a decision. That is really the point here, people! The more opportunities I can give a child to exercise their brain to make good, quality decisions, the more confident they will feel handling more complex decisions as they get older. This applies to making healthier food choices at school, finding quality friends, or being in tune with *who* and *what* is important to them each day of their life. Today, it's a treasure box, but tomorrow it may be a memory bin as they head off to college and make plans for their future career.

Select 3 mega toy themes and build on those. Growing up, my boys loved Thomas the Tank Engine toys, so we kept our train collection limited to Thomas and his friends rather than collecting from multiple train track manufacturers. As they got older, LEGOS became their favorite building blocks. This allowed them to use multiple sets from the same brand and did away with the necessity of organizing and storing different brands in separate systems. If your girls like American Girl Dolls, have them collect and add to that doll brand and its clothing and accessories instead of purchasing multiple brands. Set a limit on the types of dolls they can collect. If there are too many toy themes and mixed brands, it becomes too confusing to keep track of and organize.

Solutions for Games with Many Pieces

Packing tape to the rescue. Many games and puzzles come in cardboard boxes that are not very strong. Here's a trick I learned. When you have all the pieces gathered together, adhere clear packing tape on all the top and bottom corners of the box. The heavy duty, small dispenser style tape offered by Scotch Brand® is my top favorite for size and quality. It is not a matter of if the box will rip, it is *when*. We literally adhere tape the moment a new game set is given to protect it.

For loose sets where no organized system is provided, create your own.

1. Place all the pieces inside an appropriately sized zipper-style bag, which makes it easy for small hands to slide

closed. Ziploc® and Hefty® offer a variety of different sized zipper bags.

2. Double-check the toy's measurements to ensure it will fit in one bag before purchasing.
3. Involve your child in labeling each bag so they understand the bag and the toy set belong together.
4. Adhere clear packing tape over the label to avoid it peeling off over time. Enlarge or laminate puzzle images to have as a handy guide when trying to complete them.
5. Place games up high until your child is mature enough to keep each set organized. Toys need to be stored away for adult approval and retrieval, especially during playdate time. Otherwise, your playroom with look like an apocalypse occurred, and you will be waving a white flag in full surrender!

Inside Toys vs. Outside Toys and Treats

Personally, I feel hard sports balls can cause significant damage inside a home, so I categorize them as *outside toys* that need to be stored in the garage. I negotiated with all the boys in my family (my hubby included) that small, soft foam balls (about the size of a child's hand) could be considered *inside toys* as long as they are played with and stored in the kids sleep room and/or playroom. Nerf gun use should be discussed, and usage based on your own house rules. I allow it only their rooms, and they must wear either swim or hobby googles ... those darn bullets go everywhere

Messy crafts and other gooey goodies. Play-Doh and paints are outside toys at my house since they're a nightmare to clean up, especially if stepped into ... welcome to the jungle!

Define your snack stations. In our house, no drinks, food, or snacks are allowed in my boys' room, which keeps the carpet clean, and the critters out. The only exception to this rule was when my kids were in preschool. If they were good and quiet during nap time, I would allow them to nap in their pop-up tent with a blanket, non-spill sippy cup, and dry snack treat. Man did that little tent-and-treat scenario do the trick! Whatever mess is made, they are responsible for cleaning it up with our trusty handheld cordless Pivot Vac from Black + Decker. It is hands down the most compact, impressive, and powerful handheld vac I have ever used. Better yet, the kids have no issues cleaning up their messes when using it ... never.

Space to roam, explore, and create. One of the biggest mistakes clients make is having too much bulky furniture in a child's room or playroom rather than maximizing the existing closet storage. Avoid adding endless misfit storage solutions on the room floor since it takes away from your child's space to roam, explore, and create.

Double duty solutions. Some of my favorite toy solutions are ones that serve two purposes. For instance, for one client, we found a small working table where her child could play, and it included storage beneath—maximizing the area.

Trinkets and Treasures

Children love gathering and keeping collections of their treasures, from a unique rock Grandpa gave them to a smooshy, sticky hand earned at the local arcade or a friend's birthday party. Although most things fun and funky bring joy, all too often they transform at midnight from joy to junk. If these joyful treasures are not contained early enough, eventually a child's entire desk, dresser, or room can become a treasure box.

1. Work with your child to gather all their trinkets into one banker box. This exercise teaches altruism and decision-making and helps them prioritize their keepsakes.
2. Next, have your child select a basic shoebox or similar-sized container to house their trinkets and treasure.
3. Grab your trusty label maker and assist them with the wording and placement of a few labels to personalize their box. Crooked, straight, upside down—just let them be creative and enjoy personalizing their box with some phrases and frames from the label maker. Kids love to feel in charge when working with adults.
4. Next, tell them how many kids do not have *any* of the treasures they have. Explain that those children might enjoy having something to fill their treasure box.
5. Encourage and help them select their Top 10 most favorite-favorite-favorite treasures from the banker box to put into their treasure box.
6. If they come across anything they prefer to pass along to another child, or schoolteacher for their classroom box, then support that decision.

Under pressure: Do not force or pressure a child to make an emotional decision on their treasures. Imagine if they did that to you on your most treasured shoe, tool, or photo collection…not that easy right? You will immediately destroy their confidence and trust in you as their parent. This results in moving backward rather than forward. Skip over the more difficult decisions to find the easier ones. You can always circle back to review the inventory again and praise them on whatever progress did occur.

ASSIGN PHASE

Solutions for Toy Sets

This could be an entire book in itself since each child's room, closet, and shared living space can vary. To simplify the solution selection process, here are my top fan favorites:

Bare-Bones Budget: Gather and repurpose as many containers from your Bin of Bins, a resale shop, or even a neighbor's bulk trash. Don't laugh! When Devon was born, I scored two 3-drawer Sterilite units from a neighbor's bulk trash pick-up. I hosed them off, wiped them clean, and used them in the playroom and the pool area—and they're still going strong!

Moderate Budget: If most of your child's toy items are small, the ClosetMaid® Cube Storage Systems offers a variety of melamine finishes and fabric drawer unit styles. If you desire a more modern style, consider the Ikea® Brand KALLAX Shelving Unit System, which can be hung on the wall or stand on the floor. It's offered in neutral or vibrant colors. All bins must be clearly labeled to maintain order. Hang an organizing tag from our online collection or use natural jute to wrap a sample of the toy that should be placed inside (e.g., tie a horse on the handle of the "animal bin" to represent the theme of that bin). This helps little ones identify the contents inside until they can read labels. They will learn this type of order during clean-up time in preschool so better to start at home, to make the transition a smooth one.

Fancy-Pants Budget: The Elfa® Mesh Start-a-Stack System from The Container Store is a classic and versatile metal and mesh drawer solution. It's perfect for holding anything from small to large. You can select the height and depth of each drawer (aka runners). The system offers white or platinum mesh runners and configurations can range from 3-runner to 7-runner tall units. Custom-fit trays or mesh dividers are also available to maximize the space in each drawer further. Select a square melamine work surface to place on top or spread the units apart and purchase the rectangular desktop size so your investment can work double duty. As your child's needs grow, you can stack or swap out more units to be used as a desk and add a chair.

Storing odd-sized toys. Adding a set of bed risers can increase storage capabilities from 4–8 inches depending on the brand and stacking style. For years, I used an old drawer on wheels to house odd-shaped toys under the boy's beds or in an enclosed container.

Another favorite option of mine is using a *clear, zipper-styled garment bag* for funky shaped inside or outside toys, such as archery sets or water slides. Use duct tape or binder clips to seal the hanger top opening to prevent small parts from falling out or critters crawling in.

Stuffed Animal Intervention

Parents have promised to give me literally the most generous of gifts if I am able to work with their child to reduce their stuffed animal collection. Seeing a parent's reaction to what their child and I have achieved is the grandest gift to me. Their mouth drops open, and they stare in the room, mesmerized, like I am the Baroness Maria von Trapp in the film *Sound of Music,* teaching the kids to sing in harmony! This interaction with a child is one of my most cherished of challenges. I LOVE how it can be quite an emotional and healing time for the child, and then later, for the parent who feels pride in the child's experience.

I'll let you in on my secret. Here's the exact dialogue of how I do it:

1. Tell your child you want to do a fun game with them and all their furry friends.
2. Pinky promise none of their friends will be hurt during this game.
3. Do this at a time when you can avoid pesky distractions that can derail you.
4. Sit on the floor face to face with your child and tell them how much you love and appreciate them.
5. Talk about how much they love and appreciate their furry friends too, and how that means it is important to take good care of them, right?
6. If you love your furry friends, you will make sure they are safe and clean. But, when there are too many, you both are not able to do that, which makes both you and them sad, right?
7. Ask your child to select their Top 10 most favorite, favorite friends by lining them up in order from least to most favorite.
8. Share how lucky they are to have 10 favorite friends and how you bet there are kids out there who would love to have furry friends of their own, like kids who were

hurt in a car accident or had a house fire or who are sick in a hospital. Maybe even a grandma or grandpa who doesn't have any cute grandchildren to visit them would like some.

9. Aside from the Top 10 friends, ask your child to select which furry friends they could pass on to someone else to love and put those in a separate pile. Commend them each time they make a decision, even if it is just one friend. Kindly and patiently keep asking them as you review all the remaining furry friends.

10. Aside from the Top 10 favorites, which are next 5 favorites that they want to clean with a baby wipe and place in a clear zipper bag to "nap" under their bed while they sleep at night. Everyone needs their zzz's, right?

11. Allow your child the opportunity to swap out friends so they don't exceed a total of 15 furry friends, which may test their decision-making skills.

12. Involve your child in the dropping off/donating process. If your child wants to take a picture or video of what they kept and what they parted with for memory keeping, then do so!

13. Never, ever, ever force them to make a decision until they are ready to do so, or they will stop trusting you, and their confidence in the process will backslide tenfold.

Something more serious to ponder: What I am about to share may hurt...hurt to hear and hurt your heart, but I feel it is important enough to share, since I have seen the tremendous healing IMPACT it has had on families over the years!

I have consistently found there is a psychological reason a child has an ongoing hoarding compulsion to gather an excessive number of furry friends. It is something to be aware and mindful of, which is why I mention it. Here are a few scenarios that could come into play:

1. The parent and/or grandparent is the one who enjoys showering love on the child in the form of animals. It could be due to the adult not having a consistent source of comfort in their personal life or marriage and want to offer that in the relationship to that child.
2. The child enjoys hoarding friends based on similar reasons as the adult, emotional trauma, instability in their health or home environment or reasons not yet identified.
3. BOTH the parent and child support/enable the animal hoarding behavior based on any of the above reasons already mentioned or ones not yet identified.
4. If, after multiple attempts of Stuffed Animal Intervention and little to no progress has been made, then I suggest you seek outside support to allow the healing process to begin. Today it is stuffed animal, tomorrow it is online shopping…it is important to address and discover healthy boundaries and the emotions that feed them. I would LOVE to Skype with you both!

ACCOUNTABLE PHASE

Here are some simple ways to keep the space orderly over time:

Tidy up the room before dinner. Early on in life, my mom used to tell my sister and me, "You girls can make the biggest mess you want, as long as it is cleaned up before dinner time!"

In the beginning, we loved the creative freedom to play with our tea sets and Disney records, but then we quickly realized the extra work that meant, especially since I had to get my sister to help clean up. Eventually, as the older, OCD, organizer sister, I set the pace for the project. After a few game sets were open, I would "take charge" (not always with the nicest tone, I may add—sorry, sis!) by announcing we needed to put away some toy themes that were taken out before we begin playing with a new theme. I remember the dialogue in our playroom like it was yesterday!

Action Step: Decide if your family would like to adopt this concept or prefer to handle the cleanup after dinner, before game time, or before bedtime. This avoids increasing volumes of cluttered "layers" from one day to the next and poor, overall habit keeping.

You've conquered Toys, Trinkets, and Treasures and earned another stack of clutter-free coins to keep your organizing game strategy strong if you successfully completed the following:

Assess and Attack Phase

- ❑ Identified your child's top 3 favorite toy sets and possible organizational product solutions as well as storage locations.
- ❑ A treasure box has been identified and labeled (even if it's temporary) to be personalized or upgraded later.
- ❑ Stuffed animal intervention has occurred or is set to be done at another point in time.

Assign Phase

- ❏ Identified inside toys versus outside toys, and a location has been selected for storing crafts and gooey goodies.
- ❏ Swapped temporary labels for final ones once you and your child feel comfortable and confident all systems have been identified, and items are in their proper place in the space!

Accountable Phase

- ❏ You have implemented a "tidy up the room before dinner" or another program to keep your child's room clean and habits ongoing.

Hot Diggity-Dog…Order yourselves up a salty pretzel and warm cheese dipping sauce! You both are taking this organizing "jam" all the way downtown! Next chapter up to bat is Conquering Art, Medals, and Memory Mayhem.

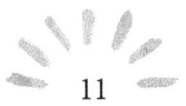

11

CONQUER ART, MEDALS, AND MEMORY MAYHEM

I have yet to meet a child who doesn't enjoy viewing their most prized art creations, school pictures, certificates, or medals that they have acquired over the years. These types of gems will continually enter your home, so it's best to decide early on whether to create a system for display or to store.

ASSESS AND ATTACK – COMBO PHASE

Banker boxes containing favorite keepsakes have already been created in previous chapters, or you used other methods. Hunt and gather from other locations to be assured all creative stragglers are found. Use all your newfound skills to power through the remaining inventory. Create a Maybe Pile of Misfits to revisit later or slide art into mailing envelopes to pass along to grandparents or loved ones.

ASSIGN PHASE
Displaying Art, Special Moments, and Medals

When Devon was young, I loved the idea of having his cherished work be the central decorative focus of his room, so I created this **Art Cable Kit System.** Use a *modern wire cable* with loop securing ferrules or, alternatively, a length of *natural jute* rope or *colorful ribbon*. Then attach the artwork with binder clips and start hanging the art. This system fits the following criteria:

- Budget-friendly: 2 long galvanized nails, hanging material of choice, binder clips of choice, and a hammer to install it.
- Easy to install without hiring help.
- Art, photos, or certificates can be protected in clear sleeves.
- 12 art pieces can be displayed on two six-foot-long kits.
- Rotation of items can be handled by your creative kiddo.
- Love this kit solution! It is FUN and DONE!

Alternative art hanging options: Hang a series of clipboards on the wall in the style vibe of their room or use a rail-style, tackless paper holder used in many teachers' classrooms.

Memory bin options: You are welcome to continue using the temporary banker box if only storing inside the home. For garage or attic storage, a hearty plastic tote with a secure lid will prevent water, moisture, or curious critters from destroying its contents. To prevent yourself and your child from storing too many bins, envision the pile 18 years in the future, and keep only the most precious memories. Eventually, they will be transferring their bins to their first apartment or home once they leave the nest … tissues, please!

Epic Organizing Adventure: Art Memory-Keeping Roadmap

Hop over to my website, **WurthOrganizing.com**, and print off the **Choose Your Own Adventure: Art Memory Keeping Roadmap.**

Review and discuss together which art-keeping adventure you choose to take. When sorting and storing keepsakes, here's a process and solutions to consider:

1. Initial sorting is done by your child, with or without your assistance, directly from their backpack.
2. Place the keepers in their clean laundry basket for direct room delivery.
3. Keepers are placed in a temporary upright three-inch magazine tote, archive box, or wall pocket in their room.
4. Once the tote becomes full, it's time for your child to purge once again, only keeping top favorites.

Hooks Make for Happy Endings

I would honestly love to give the creator of the Command Brand Hooks by 3M a big wet kiss on their cheek in gratitude for this brilliant product line, and here are my reasons why:

- Can be hung literally anywhere in a matter of seconds.
- Comes in multiple finishes, including platinum and bronze.
- Sturdy and long-lasting: holds a hand towel in our bathroom.

- Easily removes from the wall without damaging wall surfaces.
- Great for holding necklaces, lanyards, or prized medals. If you have a larger collection, use a wire kit to hang these in rainbow order. Team pics can be placed above. Ours is located in the family rec room, and we call it the "Wall of Fame."
- Hang mini flashlights near bedside to encourage reading.
- Travel-friendly when more organization is required.

ACCOUNTABLE PHASE

A generous number of keepsakes is brought home by the bagful at the end of every school year. It can be overwhelming to conquer it all. However, with more mindful methods and skills improving each month, then hopefully, the workload will feel lighter.

Action Step: Since you selected your final memory-keeping system from the Roadmap Printable, now the final push needs to happen, so the past year doesn't "spillover" to the next school year. Start by completely emptying the backpack. From snacks and supplies to papers and pencils, it's time to decide what should be trashed, restocked at home, or donated. Purge and process all remaining schoolwork into your selected system. Hang art or take pictures to cherish and toss originals. Sit together to review the school year at a glance as a family. This process can be so healing for you both to see how your child grew as a student from the start to the end of the year.

You conquered Art, Medal, and Memory Mayhem and earned another stack of clutter-free coins to keep your organizing game strategy strong if your successfully completed the following:

Assess & Attack Phase

- [ ] All art- and memory-related items have been reviewed and sorted accordingly.
- [ ] A magazine tote, archive box, or wall pocket has been discussed or installed to hold your child's schoolwork throughout the school.

Assign Phase

- [ ] You have discussed and installed a solution for displaying art, special moments, and medals, if you so desire.
- [ ] You have completed the Epic Organizing Adventure by reviewing the Art Memory Keeping Roadmap to decide your final memory storage method. That may be an Archive Box, Memory Binder Book, or in a digitally preserved format.
- [ ] Hooks have been purchased or are ready to install for holding personal items, medals, and/or flashlights.

Accountable Phase

- [ ] All end-of-year items have been reviewed, restocked, and remembered. You have set a time to reflect upon the entire school year to recap all the memories compiled together.

Way to blast this chapter to the past! Creating Homework Zones is coming up next for you gregarious gurus…You got this!

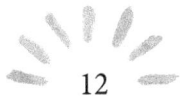

12

CREATING HOMEWORK ZONES

Having a well-organized place where your child can successfully and efficiently complete their homework or multistep school projects is a PRETTY BIG DEAL.

A well-organized homework zone needs to include structural and systematic organizing elements to increase confidence, sustain predictable order, and be easily maintained while the users are constantly starting and finishing homework or other school projects. Now, reflect back on your child's organizing personality and review these helpful tips, so together, you both can create a productive space for your child to work.

What All Kids Crave in Their Homework Zone:

- **Order.** Organized systems should be set based on age-appropriate and developmental benchmarks. If your child can maintain order while learning at school, then they can continue to do the same at home.
- **Tools.** A place to store their favorite mechanical pencil, eraser, or colored marker set, so they can quickly find these belongings.

- **Comfort.** Physically comfortable for productive, focused work.
- **Organization.** Well-defined zones are essential. They establish where in the home things belong (backpack or homework supplies), so consistent order is created. Order diminishes frustration and allows work to begin sooner rather than later.

Homework Zone Guidelines

Depending on your child and their level of responsibility, it is wise to discuss at the start of each week what is happening during the upcoming school week. Have *your child* first share what *they* know is due. Then, you can double-check whether anything was missed and determine if it needs to be mentioned *before* the due date. We will discuss planning strategies for longer-term projects later in this chapter.

- **Goals of the Space:** A successful Homework Zone is a comfortable place where your child can work. It is stocked with their favorite tools, and the space offers few distractions.
- **Need for Flexibility:** Make the most of downtime between after-school activities' pickup and drops offs. At times, one child has downtime to do homework while the other is at practice. Identify a variety of spots to work in the car, at a nearby café, or at the library, especially if wi-fi is required to access school resources.
- **Identify the Motivators:** Every human is motivated by something, and my kids are no different. Therefore, I was determined to identify what motivated my boys.

Even though Oliver is more distractible in mind, we found that listening to music while working at the computer desk kept him motivated to focus for 45 minutes. Then we would take a five-minute "snack break." On the other hand, Devon preferred to work in his comfy chair with sound dampening headphones and chose a "game break" over food.

Discuss and discover a variety of methods with your kiddo until the right combo is found so they can gradually fall into a healthy and consistent working rhythm. Today, it's *in-home work habits that lay the foundation for their future in-career work habits.*

Epic Organizing Adventure: Homework Contract Completion

Set aside time to talk with your child about what locations, solutions, and motivation combos work and don't work for them when completing their work. Then complete the Homework Contract together and sign at the bottom (or print off this page and post as a future reference).

I, _____ (aka, Clutter-Free Kiddo) _____, hereby will productively work for _____ minutes, for the following motivators:

Yummy Snack _____

Yummy Treat _____

Game Time _____

Favorite Show _____

Activity of Choice _____

If challenges occur, I will discuss with my parent; otherwise, I am fully aware that the consequences (beside my teacher's missing assignment slip…Ouch!) will be:

- ❏ No Dessert after Dinner
- ❏ No Treat in My Lunch
- ❏ Removal of Game Time
- ❏ Removal of Phone/Social

Alternative Consequence: _____
Clutter-Free Kiddo Signature _____ Date: _____
Amazing Supportive Parent _____ Date: _____

Top 3 Homework Station Tips

1. **Designate the kitchen table as the homework station and the formal dining table for family meals.** This clear division in purpose allowed me to prep meals while the kiddos did homework, and I was nearby for added support.

2. **Repurpose a small Lazy Susan for remote controls into a carousel for holding homework supplies.** This concept was sparked by the 1970s Crayola Carousel I was obsessed with using in my childhood years. Without a doubt, it really put a fun "spin" on starting homework sooner, rather than later. My boys and I

worked together to organize all of their supplies and brands to determine which ones were put in the caddy, what was kept as back stock, and what was donated.

3. **Designate Sunday night as tidy up the tables time.** It is my boys' responsibility to empty their backpacks, look through their homework folders and binders, and sort their school papers into themed piles. Once the boys have sorted everything, they let me know so we can go through the piles that need to be reviewed together. Not only are backpacks cleared out, and papers sorted for the week, but also the boys give the Homework Table a much-needed cleaning. If homework is done and lunches made for Monday, they get a thumbs up and are granted permission to frolic in free time.

Top 3 Computer and Tech Tips

1. **Designate a computer and charging station area.** In our family TV room, we turned a wall niche into our computer area. We use a small donated desk for the computer station with a dictionary nearby. A Silver Mesh 3-Pocket Wall Organizer is installed against the back wall of the niche to hold and protect iPads and laptops while being charged.

2. **Enforce a turn-off-the-tech family rule.** I suggest setting rules around tech use. That may mean all tech is to be returned to a central charging station at bedtime or parental control options are set through your service provider. Either option ensures tech can remain protected, freshly charged for the next day, and/or not used during the late evening or early morning hours.

Alternative options could be setting the home wi-fi to turn off at a certain time, parental control apps, or settings that a child would be unable to access.

3. **Rotate between reading time and tech time.** When the boys were in their early preschool and elementary years, I repurposed a small baby food jar and filled it with one quarter, two dimes, and two nickels per child. I wrote their initials on each set using tape and a Sharpie. The 60 *cents* in coins equaled 60 *minutes* in reading time. When they wanted to read for *10 minutes,* they each deposited their *initialed dime* into the Coin Jar. It made them more accountable for their reading time, and they loved managing how long they would read by popping in a coin to track it. The coin method also improved their math skills, since they learned each coin's value and added them in different ways. Now that the boys are older, we still count their time but use the kitchen microwave timer instead.

Do Not Panic! Go Around the Leaf!

In the popular Disney Pixar movie, *"A Bug's Life,"* the ants are walking and working in single file.[4] A leaf falls off a tree and lands in the middle of their path. An ant frantically screams out, *"I'm lost! I'm lost! Where's the line? We will be stuck here forever! Help!"*

The rest of the ants begin to panic. Their trusty leader, Mr. Soil, shouts out, *"Do not panic! Do not panic! We are trained professionals! Now stay calm, we are going around the leaf."*

The ants say, *"Around the leaf? I don't think we can do that".*

Mr. Soil says, *"Oh, nonsense! This is nothing compared to the twig of '93".* He guides the ants to walk around the leaf saying, *"Now, that's it, that's it, good, you're doing great! There you go, there you go! Good job, everybody!"*

Whenever either of my boys starts to freak out about some homework project, one of us will say, "Walk around the leaf! Just walk around the leaf." It makes all of us immediately burst into laughter, works every time. Stay focused and dive back into your Organizer Tool Kit.

Multistep School Projects

Every family and student dynamic for learning varies. Be patient as you determine the learning combination that works best for your child. Both my boys are taught a gifted class curriculum, so we have constant (and rigorous) deadlines throughout the year. Here's the rollout of how it all goes down, so projects get done at our house:

---

[4] Hubner, Devon. "Bug's Life Going Around the Leaf." YouTube. September 02, 2015. https://www.youtube.com/watch?v=qTQJdGp4F34.

1. **Gather required information.** When a new project is assigned, I instruct my boys to grab a pocket folder and place the project instructions and rubric sheet inside with a few pieces of lined paper.
2. **Set an early completion date.** Even though the due date is marked at the top of the paper, we write the date of the week before on the folder. A buffer is beautiful just in case the project gets ruined or someone gets sick … Life WILL happen!
3. **Overall project discussion.** I have my son write down all the physical parts needed for the project, such as poster board, paper, markers, stickers, and other items that will need to be purchased. Often, we have these discussions during car rides between school and soccer practice, so the time is spent wisely and not wastefully. We keep old composition books in the back seat for notetaking, and these can later be placed in their project folder—very helpful on sooo many levels.
4. **Detailed project discussion.** The next steps involve working with my son to discuss all the steps in the project, as well as deadlines. Some things we consider include: deciding on the topic, researching the topic, writing about the topic, editing the written work, sketching a layout for the project, printing the various elements of the project, and assembling the parts into a completed project.
5. **Use trays to organize and protect project parts.** Use a bedside serving tray or cookie sheet from the kitchen to corral all contents to keep them from becoming lost or damaged. It also makes for easier cleanup. Trays help

everyone stay organized when starting and stopping during small windows of work time.

6. **Capture the completion with a picture.** Take a picture or video of your child upon project completion for future memory keeping and just in case the project gets ruined in transit to school.

7. **Review and revise your project methods.** Review what worked well when completing the project and what areas of efficiency could be improved for the next one. This brings confidence and takes maturity each time to self-evaluate.

You've created Homework Zones and earned another stack of clutter-free coins to keep your organizing game strategy strong if you successfully completed the following:

❏ Reviewed, discussed, and identified Homework Zone Guidelines for your family home.
❏ Completed the Epic Organizing Adventure for this chapter and posted it for reference, if you so desire.
❏ Identified the location of a Homework Station and set up an efficient organizing system to keep essential supplies within easy reach during daily use (if applicable).
❏ Identified the location of a Computer or Charging Tech Station, along with an efficient organizing system for storing supportive supplies for daily use (if applicable).
❏ Worked together on a multistep project, using trays to contain its many moving parts.

❑ Reflected openly on what worked and what didn't so improvements can be made for future projects.

HUGE PRAISE for you and your organizing kiddo! Have you noticed a shift in your relationship? Your communication style together? If it hasn't developed yet, the best is yet to come as we proceed to the yummiest of chapters ... Kids in the Kitchen.

13

KIDS IN THE KITCHEN

The title of the chapter almost sounds like an oxymoron … right?

I once thought so until I became a mother. I think there's a connection between *how* a parent views this space and the *role* they see their child in it.

There is more of *everything* when you have children: more food to buy, meals to prep, lunches to make, and place settings to set, clean, and reset. At every age, there is a *role* your child can play in *each* of these tasks, and these relate to each of the Kitchen Zones I will share with you. Involving your kiddo in the kitchen serves numerous purposes *and* teaches countless and impactful life skills … more than we ever possibly considered. In the kitchen? Yuuppp … in the kitchen!

Some of my all-time family fav organizing methods and silly time-saving hacks are in this dang space. For me, the kitchen is the one place where I literally want to get in, get out, and get on with my life. Unless I am baking something creative and yummy with my boys, who are *always* allowed to lick the cake batter beaters, I only like to spend a limited amount of time in there. Otherwise, like my New York, Italian Papa used to say, "Fuhgettaboutit!"

The goal in this space is to make meals as *efficiently* as possible. To prevent backtracking, kitchens need to have designated zones for work and for storing related items. Our focus in this chapter will be on creating a kitchen and food planning structure that works for you and your child. While working together *as a family, for the family* in the kitchen, you will decide what is age-appropriate for them to handle safely.

Now that your kitchen is organized from completing the main book, make sure all the bottoms of drawers and cupboards are properly labeled. I suggest starting with the **Kitchen Theme Printable List** and give your child a grand tour of each zone. Work together on adjusting labels accordingly. You will find the following kitchen zones to identify in your own space, and then look for the Epic Organizing Adventure Jeep icons with a series of **Organizing Missions** you can embark on completing together.

- **The Serving Ware Zone:** place for storing plates, bowls, cups, and serving pieces.
- **The Cooking Zone:** place for storing the pots, pans, cooking utensils, and gadgets.
- **The Cutting Zone:** place for storing knives and cutting boards used during meal prep.
- **The Cleaning Zone:** place for storing cleaners and cloths for sanitizing surface areas.
- **The Beverage Zone:** place for storing all coffee and tea station supplies.
- **The Food Pantry Zone:** place for storing all food, baking, and backstock supplies.

The Serving Ware Zone

No matter their age, there will *always* be a role your child can play to help the family. From putting spoons in the spoon slot when in preschool to helping prepare food as they get older, there are many ways they can help and take responsibility.

Organizing Mission: Time to Empty the Dishwasher

1. Working together, empty the dishwasher and show how and where certain items are to be placed.
2. For pieces that are too dangerous or delicate for kids to handle, you can have them either leave them in the dishwasher or place them on the counter so you can safely put them away.
3. Then, set a timer and quiz each other to find certain items!

Organizing Mission: Time to Set the Table

I love to spend time decorating our family dinner table with seasonal themes and place cards for the four of us that I change nearly every month. I get a kick out of rotating placemats with charger sets with different nicely starched ironed napkins adorned with a decorative ring. It's kind of my thing.

As a child, I loved watching my mom's face light up as she took such pride in this task, and it made our family time feel special. I wanted that same magical childlike feeling and finished look to be applied to our table all year-round.

1. Involve your child as they help coordinate table themes.
2. Watch their pride as they assist in writing out the place cards, even for visiting friends for a playdate or sleepover.
3. Encourage them to put out the plates, add décor, or assist with lighting candles.
4. Discuss what simple touches make your meals together special.

The Cooking Zone

Every family has their own level of comfort and kitchen know-how for having kids help when cooking. Here are some task suggestions to try together.

Organizing Mission: Time to Cook a Meal

1. Discuss the importance of clean hands before you begin food prep.
2. Start off with helping them prepare a snack like popcorn in the microwave or basic mac and cheese from a box.
3. Read the directions and teach the math with measuring cups and spoons.
4. Enjoy the meal together and share what you each learned.
5. Clean up all cookware and wipe down working area.

The Cutting Zone

In every Kitchen Zone, the *role* your child plays depend on their age and maturity. This is particularly true in the Cutting Zone, where they need to handle food and knives properly.

Organizing Mission: Time to Prep a Meal

1. Select a fruit or vegetable of their choice for snack prep.
2. Show how to wash that type of food properly and what is the waste (for example, hulling a strawberry and discarding the stem).
3. Use a small cheese or paring knife that is comfortable for little hands when cutting and prepping food.
4. Place sliced fruit into snack containers for future lunch making smiles.
5. Clean up tools and surfaces accordingly.

The Cleaning Zone

It is amazing how anyone can learn by consistent visual example, and I have the story to prove it. When Oliver was 18 months old, I noticed from afar that he had spilled his glass of milk on the kitchen floor. He immediately waddled over to the clean rags bin, grabbed a rag, walked back to the spill, bent down putting his squishy-diaper butt high in the air, wiped the spill as best he could, and then placed the dirty rag on top of the dryer which is where it belongs.

If only I had caught the moment to share on YouTube! Regardless, I just witnessed Ollie (even though he couldn't read labels) follow in the footsteps of his fellow family members by doing this three-step action for tending to spills. The inner nerd in me just stood there with my mouth wide open and realized the tremendous power of setting a consistent example for anyone of any age!

Organizing Mission: Time to Clean Up

1. Encourage the same results with your children by having a child-friendly size bottle filled with nontoxic cleaner and rags handy for helping hands to wipe off the dining table once dishes are brought into the kitchen.

2. Consider making your own healthy mixture, like we do. Our cleaning solution is 50/50 water and vinegar plus a few drops of an antibacterial oil plus lavender oil. It's the best smelling cleaner, and my boys have used it since their preschool years to clean our glass table and countertops.

3. Show them where the table cleaning supplies are and how to use them properly.

4. Inspect their fine work and encourage them as they learn.

5. Explain how all supplies need to be properly put away. Use your nifty handheld vacuum or broom set for lingering crumbs on the floor.

Organizing Mission: Let's Talk Trash

By now, you should have labeled trash and recycle bins, so you are never asked for the rest of your human life which one is which and where it is located.

1. Show your child where the trash and/or recycle bins are located inside your home *and* outside your home, so they know where to properly dispose of *both* when the inside bins need to be emptied.
2. Eventually, you can have them roll the bins out to the sidewalk or to the building basement for weekly pickup.
3. Label the tops of all cans or drawers so they are clearly marked.
4. Discuss what and how items can be recycled (for example, washing out a glass jar and separating the metal lid).
5. The more you involve kids in household duties, the more they will appreciate all that is needed to maintain a clean home and planet ... give each other high-fives for healthy choices!

The Beverage Zone

Here's an easy area where your kiddo can help out at *any* age, from filling cups with water and ice for delivering to the dinner table to putting away coffee mugs when they are older.

Organizing Mission: Time to Match Cups to Lids

1. Pull out all the cups and lids.
2. Ask your child to match up all the sets.
3. Put all the "mystery pieces" into a labeled Ziploc bag.
4. Over a few dish loads, donate misfit sets accordingly.

The Food Pantry Zone

It's finally time to give your child the grand tour of the pantry, fridge, and freezer, so they can help put away groceries, prep for meals, make lunches, and prepare snacks that are age-appropriate.

Organizing Mission:
Pantry Review and Resolve by Labeling

EVERYTHING MUST BE LABELED. It's the #1 most costly mistake made on an Organizing Mission! How can your kids put their school snack bars in the basket that holds them if it isn't clearly labeled? Everything needs to be labeled, whether food containers with bulk foods (such as rice) or baskets that hold food themes (such as school snacks).

Let me repeat for emphasis . . .

EVERYTHING MUST BE LABELED. How can other family members or hired helpers assist with *anything* meal planning related, especially if certain foods are only for those with allergies or intolerances, if items are not properly labeled?

1. Review each shelf of the pantry together
2. Are there any food themes that are not clearly labeled?
3. What areas need improvement for smaller helping hands?
4. Jot down what product, label, or solution can resolve them and implement it as a team.
5. Celebrate with the child's choice of treat!

Budgeting for your family's groceries. When Phil and I were newly married and extremely broke in our very early twenties, we took a Bible study that followed the Dave Ramsey budgeting program, where we learned to budget monies and become debt-free. We created a basic Excel spreadsheet of all our incoming and outgoing expenses, then decided which money themes would be paid for in cash each month.

- **Dividing funds per month.** At the start of each month, I would freely skip on over to the bank, pull out funds for my cash-only categories, come home, and divide the grocery monies into two piles, one for the first half of the month and the other for the second half of the month. I had quickly learned that we lived like kings and queens the first half of the month and then like peasants for the last half of the month, eating random food and leftover combinations that even our dog would walk away from.

- **Dividing funds per week.** Things turned a corner in many ways when I divided the grocery monies into four weeks. That meant I would shop and buy fresh food once a week, more like a European and not an American. As we got older and more debt-free, it was easier to budget for quarterly bulk shopping at our local Costco, because I would ration some funds each week knowing we could apply them for quarterly shopping trips there.

- **Discuss the importance of a food budget.** Once I had the boys, they were involved with my monthly trips to the bank. They truly enjoyed it, because it felt like they were involved in a real-life Monopoly Game.

They helped me sort all the cash for the month on the dining table and were rewarded for their responsibility and stewardship for counting and clipping each category together. Life got very real, very quickly, since they knew the exact amount we were able to spend each week.

Meal Planning – Make it Simple and Savory

Like a tornado in Kansas, I was that overwhelmed by all the recipes and meal options flying around me, from written family recipes to magazine tear-outs or online printouts. I needed a grounded game plan so, with no further ado, allow me to introduce you to the **Family Recipe Binder Book Printable** found on my website.

I have already done the hardest part and know it will be well worth the effort put forth. I also have a printable for Meal Planning and a shorter printable for Baking. Organizing your recipes is an easy project you can tackle over time, so no pressure to tackle it now. Here are some handy guidelines to keep you from what I call … turning your brain into "mental mash potatoes."

Guideline No. 1 - Acknowledge and announce to all family members that your home kitchen is NOT a restaurant kitchen. In our home, if any family member desires customized meals due to excessive personal pickiness, they are more than welcome to use their own energies to cook it, clean it, or find it (in the form of a healthy leftover option in the fridge).

Alternative Options: We are what I respectfully call a *special foods family,* since the list of food allergies and intolerances is vast and exhausting. To avoid separate meal insanity, certain foods are put *on the side* in glass bowls. This simplifies prepping and serving for the people who can consume some foods, but not others and for more particular eaters.

Guideline No. 2 - Designate meal themes to each day of the week. I adopted this brilliant concept from a home school client of mine who did this in their home, and we have loved it ever since. Based on your family size and schedule, you may elect to double portions of a meal one day, and then leftovers can be eaten for lunch or dinner the day after.

<u>Mexican Monday</u>: any Mexican dish from tacos to quesadillas.

<u>Tuna Tuesday</u>: fish-focused meals from ahi tuna to salmon burgers with rice and side salad.

<u>Panini Wednesday</u>: panini with salad in the summer or swap out the salad for soup to make a cozy winter meal. I use my waffle maker and olive oil for grilling the sandwiches, which are also great leftovers.

<u>Italian Thursday</u>: from lasagna to pasta with sliced veggies/ sausage.

<u>BBQ Friday</u>: grilled chicken, burgers, or hotdogs, served with homemade fries or roasted vegetables.

<u>Leftovers Saturday</u>: everyone eats on their own from any leftover food in the fridge. Fresh vegetables are sliced and sautéed before expiring.

<u>Pizza Night Sunday</u>: usually there is an ongoing event from past bible studies to games or school projects, so this is an easy dinner to make, eat, and clean up.

Guideline No. 3 - Adopt a zero food waste program. When health issues arose, we transitioned to a cleaner eating lifestyle. Now, during the first half of the week, we chop and store a jumbo salad to serve as the main meal or side dish. Any leftovers are grilled to avoid food waste. Lunches for the next two days are prepped following dinner time to maximize kitchen time and clean-up efficiency. Decide what food prep and themes work for you and your lifestyle.

Guideline No. 4 - Decide how you will hunt and gather food.

1. Designate your food planning day.
2. Grab a clipboard and attach my neat-o Food Shopping List (or create your own).
3. Keep your weekly budget in mind as you mark the basic staple foods to purchase.
4. Look at your scheduled events for the coming week, and plan meals for each day of the week.
5. Double a recipe when you can, so you can either have more leftovers or freeze a meal to save time later.
6. Now, decide HOW you will gather the food.

Shopping in the grocery store. I love adding a fun twist by turning everyday activities into foundational life skills, so this is what we did in the grocery store.

1. The younger child crossed the item off the grocery list on the clipboard (of course, with an attached pen so it wouldn't drop 100 times over).
2. The older child compared the *price per ounce* to decide if a smaller quantity of a brand was a better value than the larger size.

3. As items are placed in the cart, generously round up the price of *each* item to include tax, so you stay within budget before final checkout. We always *rounded up* a product's price, and we would literally fist pump at checkout when we were within a dollar. We do love being savvy shoppers!
4. If you move to a restrictive diet due to allergies and intolerances, your child can also be required to read the ingredients on labels as well.

Going hardcore. Back in the day, I was historically known for walking into stores with my cash and leaving my wallet with credit cards in the car to avoid further temptation. Sometimes folks in line would get annoyed, while others were inspired by my method. The bottom-line was that I needed to steward the money I was given and eat the food I was purchasing.

Shopping Online. As the boys grew older, our businesses grew larger, and weekend time became more precious. For only $5.95, Phil and I began ordering our food online using Clicklist.com, offered through our local Kroger and Fry's. All groceries were ordered online Saturday and picked up using curbside pickup on Sunday post-church and weekly car wash drive-through. We discovered an impressive savings in cost, time, and efficiency. If an item wasn't in stock, the store gave us a similar replacement for free and also often included other new promotional products!

Guideline No. 5 - Everyone has a role to play. Upon returning home from the store, Phil is now "off duty" because he does the meal planning and online food ordering. The boys and I unload *all* the groceries and put them *all* away. Devon usually takes cereal and snack chip duty by opening all bags and boxes and unloading them into our OXO Good Grips POP Canister Sets, while Ollie prefers to dole out all the veggies and trail mixes into twist-on snack cups (called freezer jars), made by Ball® Jars, for everyone to use for the week.

I handle washing and prepping the remaining foods into our food containers. All recyclables are put away, and the trash is taken out. We are now ready to take on a busy week of school, work, and soccer. The whole process takes about an hour, but we all can honestly say it is so worth it. During the week, our turnaround times are fast, and we are all grateful that we spent time prepping so we can move forward, stress-free with healthy options. The boys also have an entirely new perspective and appreciation for what it takes to feed a family—budgeting, planning, buying, storing, eating, and cleaning up. When we eat out, they are so very grateful and understand all that goes into creating a meal!

Guideline No. 6 - Create a family table tradition. Okay, this family tradition of ours might sound super creamy Velveeta cheesy, but hey, so is our family. You may want to tweak the tradition a little to fit your family or create your very own!

When the boys were in preschool, we wanted to encourage *all* family members (not just the talkative ones, like me) to share about their day at dinner time. One day, we came up with the concept of having a *Table Leader*. The leader is responsible for opening the meal in prayer and asking each family member how their day was … what was good or frustrating about it.

Once the table leader has asked all family members about their day, then on a count of 1, 2, 3, the interviewed family members shout out in unison, in any type of voice, to the leader, "How was your day, table leader?" I know its cheddar cheesy, but it makes us all bust out the silly smiles, especially on the days that didn't go so well. It definitely lifts our spirits.

You've fully involved your Kids in the Kitchen and earned another stack of clutter-free coins to keep your organizing game strategy strong if you successfully completed the following:

- ❑ Understood the importance that efficiency, function, and the specific placement of food and food prep inventory can have on your daily tasks.

You have shown your child the following Kitchen Zones and completed the Organizing Missions within each one:

The Serving Ware Zone:
- ❑ Organizing Mission: Time to Empty the Dishwasher
- ❑ Organizing Mission: Time to Set the Table

The Cooking Zone:
- ❑ Organizing Mission: Time to Cook a Meal

The Cutting Zone:
- ❑ Organizing Mission: Time to Prep a Meal

The Cleaning Zone:
- ❑ Organizing Mission: Time to Clean Up
- ❑ Organizing Mission: Let's Talk Trash

<u>The Beverage Zone:</u>
- ❑ Organizing Mission: Time to Match Cups to Lids

<u>The Food Pantry Zone:</u>
- ❑ Organizing Mission: Pantry Review and Resolve
- ❑ You have tripled-checked that everything in the pantry is labeled or have plans to complete it.
- ❑ You have set a budget for your family's groceries and either divided category funds by month or week.
- ❑ You've discussed the importance of a food budget with your child.
- ❑ You understand the importance of making Meal Planning simple and savory and have either created a Recipe Binder Book Binder or your own meal planning methods.

You are aware and have either completed or plan to complete the following Kitchen Guidelines:

- ❑ Guideline No. 1: Acknowledged and announced to all family members that your home kitchen is NOT a restaurant kitchen.
- ❑ Guideline No. 2: Designated a meal plan for the week.
- ❑ Guideline No. 3: Adopted a zero-food-waste program.
- ❑ Guideline No. 4: Decided how you will hunt and gather food.
- ❑ Guideline No. 5: Discussed what everyone's role is to play during and after grocery shopping, unpacking, and food prep.

❏ Guideline No. 6: Refreshed an old family tradition or started a new one to cherish your valuable dinner time together.

You both are in your FINAL ROUND of your Organizing Adventure together … this is mega progress! Let's execute our final organizing play of the day in the next chapter … Laundry Load Line Up: How Kids Can Tackle It.

14

LAUNDRY LOAD LINE UP: HOW KIDS CAN TACKLE IT

Just like a sports game, laundry needs a solid strategy and game plan in order to score big for the win! I never understood the massive role laundry plays in a parent's life until I became a mother. It was above overwhelming and beyond never-ending. Formulating more efficient systems for the entire laundry process was a massive focus of mine as a first-time mom. It wasn't only for my sense of sanity. I knew it would benefit the overall consistent flow and function of my home and would teach my boys excellent life skills.

A consistent Laundry Room Line Up plays an important *role* for a child. Here are a few reasons it's important to have them join in:

- ✓ Much like meal planning, it teaches your child that *everyone* on the family team has a *role, a position to play*, and an expected *responsibility* to care for their clothes and personal belongings.
- ✓ The more they are involved, the more their head will be in the game, and the more organized they will become overall.

- ✓ They will respect and appreciate the time invested in their possessions and learn the importance of teamwork.
- ✓ They will care for and appreciate their possessions properly and feel pride once tasks are completed.
- ✓ They will ultimately need to do it independently, as an adult.

Let's get this space organized, so the laundry is done efficiently, and you have more free time to do things, like drink your morning cup of coffee while it is still hot … what a concept!

ATTACK AND ASSIGN COMBO PHASE

Hopefully, you have already transformed your Laundry Room using the methods taught in *Ignite the Organizer in You*. Now, you are ready to give your kiddos a grand tour of the space.

Top 12 Laundry Guidelines Recap

I get lit up like Christmas when mothers share with me how much my guidelines impacted their lives and involved the family in new ways. Here's a quick recap of my **Laundry Guidelines:**

Guideline No. 1 - Decide your laundry schedule. Tell your child when you're doing laundry, so they can either help prep, place, or deliver their clothes to you.

Guideline No. 2 - Your *dirty* clothes hamper needs to be separate from your *clean* clothes basket. Each product serves totally separate purposes, so mixing them avoids any dirty clothes confusion for kids and clean clothes delay in them putting it away.

Guideline No. 3 - Start using my magical mesh bag laundry system. If I were to be remembered decades from now in the Organizing History Hall of Fame (if there isn't one, there should be), I would want to be most noted for this solution. The Whitmor® Brand Wash Mesh Bag Sets are designed for washing delicates, but I use them for housing undies and socks *per family member.* This mesh sack system is a true family life-changer!

- **Identify each family member with a colored ribbon.** Have your child select their own color/pattern to personalize their bag. Knot the ribbon multiple times through the zipper hole.
- **For adults only.** My sack is used to corral my socks, undies, and bras (be sure to hook the straps together to avoid the hooks getting tangled in the mesh bag). Phil uses his for his dress and athletic socks.
- **For kiddos only.** When Oliver arrived, his identifying ribbon was doggie prints. I used my labeler to put his name on the flat tops of the two binder clips that held up his *open sack* which was placed on the *outside* of their shared hamper. Devon's identifying ribbon was green striped, and his clips were labeled with his name as well. My clients' kiddos think it is the coolest thing ever that they have their names on the binder clips and their very own sack with a ribbon color they select.
- **Don't overstuff your bag.** Explain to your child the bag needs about 40% to move around to clean its contents. Place at least 2–3 back-up mesh sacks with identifying ribbons at the bottom of the hamper, so the system continues no matter what.

Guideline No. 4 - Stains are a pain, but Dreft® is the best. My kids know that if they get a really bad stain (like spaghetti sauce) on their clothes that they need to put that item on the laundry room counter to alert me so we can then handle it. Apply detergent generously to the garment, rub into the fabric to lift stain, place in a mixing bowl, fill with water to cover garment, and soak overnight. Gasp with your child at the magic of stain removal in the morning.

- **Have Dreft, will travel.** Everyone knows to do the same when traveling. You can just let the item soak overnight in the hotel sink.

Guideline No. 5 - Decide what to hang dry and where. The boys know to grab *their* hangered shirts from *their* labeled section, which is marked with a Xangar clothes divider on our InterMetro® laundry cart.

Guideline No. 6 - Decide what to dry in the dryer. The rest of our bottoms are tossed in the dryer. From jammies to jeans to athletic shorts and, of course, all our family's magical mesh sacks!

Guideline No. 7 - Laundry basket intervention. In the main book, I discussed in great detail why I prefer using Whitmor's soft woven strap basket with supportive wire construction. Here are a few of the reasons.

- **Just the right size.** It is quick to empty, comfortable for a child to slide or hand carry, and compact enough to store for multiple purposes.
- **Labeled by family member.** Makes putting away volume more manageable, and it's easier to find an item when divided by member.

- **Acts as a catchall for dual deliveries.** My boys' baskets act as a catchall for toothpaste for their bathroom, random toys, and even keepsake schoolwork placed in protective sleeves to be either hung up on their art cable kit or placed in the Memory Tote.
- **For those who prefer folding and piling laundry.** This system is only successful if you and/or your family are dedicated team players and immediately put laundry away. Otherwise, it creates more complications than resolutions, remaining dusty and dirty again.

Guideline No. 8 - Transfer items from the dryer to each family member's basket. We literally just chuck it all in the basket, dried hanger items are folded in half on top, and then it's time for that family member to get going on delivery.

Guideline No. 9 - Place hanger-themed items in rainbow-colored order in their respective themed sections. Touchdown! Kids can score big on this one and have the task done in a matter of minutes.

Guideline No. 10 - Place folded themed items in rainbow order in their respective shelves or drawer. Remember to position the item *finished edge up* so clothes can be seen in one glance, instead of just seeing what lies on the top of the stack. Kids really like to find what they are looking for quickly. By now, the tops of your child's drawer sections should be nicely labeled to guide you along the way!

Guideline No. 11 - Return laundry basket to its proper position in the laundry room. My kids want playtime? No problem ... if their laundry basket is emptied and returned to its lawful laundry position! If I find them complaining about housework or bickering with each other, I have them empty *their sibling's* basket instead. The feisty fumes settle down real quick while helping another family member, then another. It doesn't matter who, we are *all* a family, *all* one team, and *all* need to *support* one another following the *same* game plan.

On a Bare-Bones Budget? No problem! Assemble and add a decorative label or use a colorful strip of duct tape to label a banker box per family member. A Banker Box is about the same size as the woven basket and also offers sides handles. Yes! Upgrade your box to a basket when budget permits! It is more important to implement the laundry system than delay its start due to budget. The system is what produces the resolution, not the product.

ACCOUNTABLE PHASE

The Laundry Load Line Up program only works if you and your family stay accountable to one another and make it a weekly priority. Kids will quickly realize that they are giving themselves more work by tossing clean clothes in the hamper versus putting them where they belong when they are held responsible. The overall laundry workload can rotate responsibilities when heavy schoolwork at times take priority. One family member may support the other, knowing deadlines are coming up and, man, are they ever-so-grateful. I am included just as much in the rotation for support; writing this book took such diligence over the years!

Top 3 Laundry Lifestyle Ideas Recap

In closing, I thought it would be helpful to recap my **Top 3 Laundry Lifestyle Ideas,** which *reduce* our laundry loads per family member, while *increasing* our productivity.

- **Lifestyle Idea No. 1 – Select one pajama set for the week.**
- **Lifestyle Idea No. 2 – Select one bath and face towel for the week and use one hand towel per day.**
- **Lifestyle Idea No. 3 – Adopt the mesh sack system for sports.** If my kids don't properly maintain their soccer sacks, they will need to explain to coach why they are dressed in school clothes rather than a practice uniform. It only takes one embarrassing experience, and they become more mindful moving forward.

You've implemented a Laundry Load Line Up and earned your stack of clutter-free coins to keep your organizing game strategy strong if you successfully completed the following:

- ❑ You have given your child a grand tour of the laundry room, so they now know the locations of a variety of potential themes.
- ❑ You and your organizing kiddo understand the *role* a consistent Laundry Room Line Up plays for a child and its *level of importance*, so they can tackle it.
- ❑ You have reviewed and/or adopted one or more of the laundry guideline suggestions.
- ❑ You have considered and/or adopted one or more of the laundry lifestyle suggestions.

You and your organizing kiddo can officially declare yourselves "gurus" now that you have successfully completed each chapter and kept your organizing game plan super solid.

Way to ignite the organizer who sparked skills within you! From this day forward, may you feel the powerful force that organizing plays in your life and realize the importance of keeping its glowing energy burning bright, bright ... BRIGHT!

MATTERS
—— OF ——
REFERENCE

15

THE COACHING CORNER: A FEW QUICK WINS TO CONQUER ANYTIME

How do you teach a child to write their name? Tracing one letter together at a time! How do you untangle years of compiling clothes and keepsakes? One drawer at a time!

I totally get you! Putting your heart, mind, and hands together is not meant to be a daunting process. I did not design the book to make you and your child feel overwhelmed and frozen in frustration. No, thank you!

If you are feeling inspired to take action at ANY time while reading this book, or if you need to take a break from one chapter before moving to another, I've created a few quick-win projects that can be completed in a very, very short amount of time!

These projects are designed for you to be both creative and efficient. They give you a chance to crank out a simple, yet productive, project that you can proudly brag about to each other or use to inspire other families to follow suit on our social media. We would LOVE to do the happy dance right along WITH YOU!

Time to turn up the tunes! Reference this chapter ANY time either of you needs a confidence boost or needs my help in the coaching corner!

Let's Get Your Hearts Right

The deeper we examine ourselves, the better we can define and organize the life we want. When we turn the spotlight off products and direct ourselves inward, we tend to gravitate toward healthier, clutter-free lives. Organizing products are wonderful and give us solutions with style and vision, but that is only one part of the organizing process.

At times, it can be physically and mentally exhausting, but your inner organizer and organizer child have been ignited. You know that following the steps in the proper order is the only way the process works.

Moving forward, review your list of "whys" that you checked in the introduction. Share with your child your efforts to become more organized as their parent or how you want to teach them to be more organized as a child. Your unique list of whys is what will persuade your hearts and heads so your hands can make it happen together.

Are you both ready to commit to this new way of feeling?

❏ *Yes, we are!*

Let's Get Your Minds Right

Everyone, everywhere around the world, juggles and struggles with daily challenges as a family. Just like you, they are trying to raise a family, care for loved ones, have successful careers, and keep a well-ordered home. When you add more family members (furry friends, too) with mental, emotional, or physical disabilities, the challenges escalate.

Are you both ready to commit to this new way of thinking?

❏ *Yes, we are!*

Let's Get Your Hands Right

Let's dial back expectations and anxieties. Instead, turn up your confidence with an easy 3-Wins-in-3-Days-Challenge using your Organizer Tool Kit:

Quick Win #1 – Clean out your child's sport bag in 15 minutes

1. Empty the bag's contents onto a clean table.
2. Wipe everything down with a baby wipe or cleaning cloth.
3. Toss the trash and recycle the recyclables.
4. Gather snacks, lip balm, sunscreen, and meds together.
5. Divide up uniforms into mesh bags to be laundry ready.
6. Divide up and label uniform accessories into a clear zipper bag.
7. Discuss and decide any essentials that their bag is missing.
8. Identify a consistent location for the bag to be stored.

Quick Win #2 – Clean out your child's backpack in 30 minutes

1. Empty the bag's contents onto a clean table.
2. Wipe everything down with a baby wipe or cleaning cloth.
3. Toss the trash and recycle the recyclables.

4. Clip together important papers that can be processed later.
5. Secure tech-related gear with a rubber band.
6. Gather snacks, mints, lip balm, and meds together.
7. Relocate unnecessary items to your car, office, or elsewhere.
8. Add any essentials that your child is missing.
9. Smile wide and with confidence because of what you both just accomplished!

Quick Win #3 – Create a Toy Manual Binder Book in 30 minutes

You may laugh out loud on this one, but I must admit, it was one of our top favorite organizing systems we created very early on, especially because it seriously ROCKED!

1. Grab a three-ring binder.
2. Place clear protective sleeves inside, then label the front and spine.
3. Slide all building manuals/toy instruction sheets inside.
4. For the smaller manuals, hole punch each booklet and secured each set by size with a chrome book ring.
5. For ripped or missing instructions, print them off from the toy manufacturer website.
6. Keep everything organized until the day the set is donated or sold. We recommend your kiddo be involved in either process.

Final Thoughts

Have you referred to this chapter frequently? Are you still having difficulty completing the three organizing challenges? Here are next steps to help:

Reach out to us directly through the contact form at **WurthOrganzing.com**, and schedule a complimentary consultation or future coaching session. We will celebrate victories and overcome challenges together. You and your child are no longer in this alone because your family will be able to lean on me until you are able to stand strong on your own.

Like we always say …

Happy Days Come Through Organized Ways!

Resource Guide

All printables and products referenced in this book can be found at: WurthOrganizing.com

Bust Out and Build Your Organizing Tool Kit

- ❏ Brother PT – 1890 Label Maker
- ❏ Office Depot/OfficeMax Brand Banker Boxes

How to R.O.C.K. at Discipline

- ❏ R.O.C.K. Method Printable

Daily Systems and Rhythms

- ❏ Routine Chore Chart
- ❏ Command Brand Picture Hanging Strips
- ❏ Behavior Modification Chart

Kids' Room

- ❏ Drop Box Photo Storage App
- ❏ Mega Expand-a-Shelf 3-Tier
- ❏ Elfa, Avera, and Laren Closet Solutions
- ❏ Kids Clutter-Free Closet Checklist
- ❏ Clothing Tag Theme Printable
- ❏ Xangar Closet Spacers
- ❏ Joy Mangano Slimline Hangers

- ❏ The Home Edit Clear Shelf Divider
- ❏ Sterilite Shoebox and Drawer Solutions
- ❏ ClosetMaid Cube Storage Systems
- ❏ Ikea KALLAX Shelving Unit System
- ❏ Elfa Mesh Drawer Start-a-Stack System

Toys, Trinkets, and Treasures

- ❏ Scotch Brand heavy duty packing tape
- ❏ Ziploc and Hefty Brand zipper bags
- ❏ Black + Decker - Lithium Pivot Cordless vacuum

Conquer Art, Medals, and Memory Mayhem

- ❏ Choose Your Own Adventure: Art Memory Keeping Roadmap
- ❏ Command Brand Hooks by 3M

Creating Homework Zones

- ❏ Silver Mesh 3-Pocket Wall Organizer

Kids in the Kitchen

- ❏ Kitchen Themed Printable List
- ❏ Family Recipe Binder Book Printable
- ❏ Food Shopping List
- ❏ OXO Good Grips POP Canister Set
- ❏ Ball (Bernardin) Plastic Freezer Jars

Laundry Load Line Up

- ❑ Whitmor Laundry Mesh Bags
- ❑ Dreft Newborn Liquid Detergent
- ❑ Xangar Closet Spacers
- ❑ InterMetro Laundry Cart
- ❑ Whitmor Woven Strap Basket

A Thousand Thanks

No, really! Thank you for your kind investment in purchasing this book and all the time you and your child devoted to reading it. It came directly from my heart as a parent in the hopes of immediately moving yours. Please share freely with others.

I would love to hear how the teaching and organizing methods you learned have impacted you both! Your feedback not only helps make improvements for future books but also pays it forward by impacting many family readers not yet found.

Find out about upcoming books, events, and workshops by registering for my monthly **Teachable Tips Newsletter** via my website: **WurthOrganizing.com.**

It would make my day glow brighter if you would snap a shot of you and child with the book. Using **#ignitetheorganizerinyou** and **#ignitetheorganizerinyourchild**, share what you learned on any of our social sites. By staying connected, we can keep your inner fire burning bright, and together we can ignite the hearts and heal the homes of hundreds more!

Happy Days Come Through Organized Ways!

Danielle

Acknowledgements

To the talented team at Niche Pressworks, Nicole and Kim, it is because of your immense knowledge, expertise and loving guidance that I was able to create this companion guide. A part of you both is in every page I read.

To Rose, I will forever be grateful to you for taking this journey with me over the past two and a half years. Lastly, thank you to Dr. Lynne Kenney for writing my foreword and supporting my mission of helping and healing families. You are a woman of many talents, and I am grateful to have had the privilege of working with you and gaining wisdom from you over these past 10 years.

ABOUT THE AUTHOR

DANIELLE WURTH is the founder and CEO of Wurth Organizing as well as a professional organizer, speaker, bestselling author, and self-proclaimed recovering perfectionist. Since 2007, she and her team of organizing gurus have used her psychology-based approach to transform the lives of over one thousand individuals, families, and businesses. Her mindful and easy-to-implement organizing methods teach the benefits of living a healthy, intentional, and organized lifestyle.

Danielle's sole purpose and the inspiration for her work involve guiding clients to thrive and to reach their absolute best potential in both their homes and personal lives. All too often, she has found clients were focusing on fancy solutions before examining their habits and their actual needs. She helps them to understand why past methods and solutions have failed and teaches them what to do to overcome frustrations and lead the happier, healthier home and personal lives they always craved.

She is honored to be the only Official Brand Partner for the Container Store in Metro Phoenix with work featured in *HGTV Magazine, Real Simple* magazine, and *The List* television show. She is a former columnist for *InRecovery* magazine and a contributor to Fox 10 News and Channel *3 Good Morning Arizona. Ignite the Organizer in You* is Danielle's first book and *Ignite the Organizer in Your Child* is the companion book, geared towards parents and school-aged kids.

She lives in Scottsdale, Arizona, with her handsome hubby and her two soccer-loving sons. You will find her embracing her inner soccer mom at every game, cheering them on!

Your child's life is … Wurth Investing in.

Your child's life is … Wurth embracing today.

Your child's life is … Wurth Organizing!

WurthOrganizing.com

www.ingramcontent.com/pod-product-compliance
Lightning Source LLC
Chambersburg PA
CBHW050316120526
44592CB00014B/1936